Giovanni Ercolani

The Maidan Museum

Preserving the Spirit of Maidan.
Art, Identity and the Revolution of Dignity

With a foreword by Chris Farrands

*Thank you "Maestro",
with friendship, esteem and
deep gratitude
your Giovanni*

Giovanni Ercolani

THE MAIDAN MUSEUM

Preserving the Spirit of Maidan.
Art, Identity and the Revolution of Dignity

With a foreword by Chris Farrands

ibidem
Verlag

Bibliografische Information der Deutschen Nationalbibliothek

Die Deutsche Nationalbibliothek verzeichnet diese Publikation in der Deutschen Nationalbibliografie; detaillierte bibliografische Daten sind im Internet über http://dnb.d-nb.de abrufbar.

Bibliographic information published by the Deutsche Nationalbibliothek

Die Deutsche Nationalbibliothek lists this publication in the Deutsche Nationalbibliografie; detailed bibliographic data are available in the Internet at http://dnb.d-nb.de.

ISBN-13: 978-3-8382-1763-5

© *ibidem*-Verlag, Stuttgart 2023

Alle Rechte vorbehalten

To my father and to my mother:
Dr. Mario Rosario Ercolani
Prof. Carla Carmen Pellegrini

Abstract

This research examines the relation between art produced during the so-called *Revolution of Dignity – Maidan Events* (Kyiv, Ukraine, November 21, 2013 – February 23, 2014) and the mission of the Maidan Museum (short for: 'National Memorial of the Heavenly Hundred Heroes and Revolution of Dignity Museum', Kyiv, Ukraine) born from the ashes of Euromaidan to preserve the 'Spirit of Maidan'.

The Maidan events, defined as the Maidanization process, produced a post-colonial discourse-language, a new apolitical ideology based on the concepts of dignity and Ukrainianness; generated symbols, social myths, and collective imaginary; triggered the 'Spirit of Maidan' that changed the consciousness of the participants in the demonstrations; and functioned as a ritual of intensification-aggregation-initiation-passage, in which the identity of new Ukraine was shaped.

In this transformative process, in which the human being is seen as an 'animal identitarium' struggling, defending, and fighting for his/her own identity, artists played a crucial role in assembling the main elements of the post-Maidan Ukrainian identity (homo Maidan), were able to empower the whole movement with concrete ideas, and finally reworked objects, symbols, and music already present in the Ukrainian DNA through a process of meaningization, symbolization, mythization, canonization, sacralization, and interpellation.

This volume is based on interviews with artists who dramatically participated in the Maidan events and on fieldwork at the Maidan Museum, and unfolds and identifies the main elements, emotions, expectations, and motivations of the relation of art creation and Ukrainian post-Maidan identity formation based on the 'Spirit of Maidan'.

Therefore, this research: defines 'Maidan' as a social myth; discloses and identifies those artistic elements – symbols and archetypes – which were produced during the Revolution of Dignity and played a key role in the 'Maidanization process'. By the latter is meant the meaning the combination of the emerging mythification process with the Maidan Societal Securitization Process, which as a result created the 'Spirit of Maidan'; and examines the circumstances surrounding the creation of the mission and role of the Maidan Museum.

The conclusion confirms that Maidan is a myth and that the Maidan Musem is a unique case of a Memorial Museum dedicated to the preservation of the Revolution of Dignity's objects, to the spread of the emancipatory message of the 'Spirit of Maidan'; while remaining an active agent and cultural mediator in the definition and formation of the post-Maidan Ukrainian identity and cultural policy of Ukraine.

Key words: Maidan, art, identity, myth, ritual, animal identitarium, collective imaginaries, Spirit of Maidan, Maidanization process, anthropological gaze.

Contents

Foreword

Giovanni Ercolani's study of the Maidan Museum is in important respects an innovative study in social anthropology. It also has a wider significance, because its subject of study, the Maidan Museum in Kyiv, has taken on a greater significance even than those who created it imagined, because of the events of 2022. Ercolani explains for himself the innovations he makes in methods and philosophy of study in the book, and this Foreword will not replicate that. But it does try to set the book in wider contexts. In doing so it also makes the case that the book is more significant and less recondite than its author rather modestly suggests. Ercolani writes as a specialist in anthropology, and the book is presented as a study in that field. But he is highly qualified in both anthropology and political science and international relations, having MA and PhD degrees in both fields. And he began academic life as a linguist, with qualifications in Oriental languages specialising in Turkish; he is now fluent in more languages than I can count. Unquestionably, this book also reflects a continuing concern with the meanings and ambiguities of language and language use, including the ways in which people speaking and writing in different contexts switch codes and patterns of meanings, often without any great awareness that the code switching — as in almost all of James Joyce's writing — creates wholly new meanings in turn.

The wider contexts this Foreword opens up are, first of all, the political and cultural situation, secondly, the historic settings which help to explain some of the ambiguities of Ukraine's situation between Europe, Poland, Russia, the Black Sea, and between various versions of Christianity. Thirdly, it asks questions about the ways in which museums and other institutions memorialise not just the past, but also the very recent present, the lived experience of men and women for whom memories are not easily captured in the serious, heavy blocks of stone and concrete which make up the traditional nineteenth century idea of how the past is summarised and re-presented. Recent efforts at creating a 'present past' in popular museums, not least in the Holocaust Museums in Berlin and Washington DC, but also in many other institutions, provided examples from which the creators of the Maidan Museum learned. But that effort was primarily the result of a popular movement. It still encapsulates the immediacy of the first efforts to commemorate the events in 2013/2014. Then, ordinary people across Ukraine took to the streets to overthrow a government which they saw as undermining opportunities for democratic change and freedom from corruption, as well as from Moscow's heavy hand. 107 people died then: the Maidan Museum commemorates their lives. But it does much more than that, and what more it does is the main focus of Ercolani's analysis.

It may be useful to note from the start that the reader not familiar with the Maidan Museum can find a great deal of material easily available online, including material from the museum itself (at maidanmuseum.org) and on Youtube, including a lecture by Ercolani himself, as well as other explanations and debates in English and Ukrainian. Included in this material are virtual tours of the museum as it currently exists, as well as the full plans for the future permanent building.

The war in Ukraine which began on 24 February 2022 is a culture war. It is, of course, being fought with military means, and it has military and economic objectives as well as cultural goals. But the cultural aims Russia's invasion strives to achieve are at least as important as any others. The Maidan Museum stands in a central place in the cultural conflict between Russia and Ukraine, and by extension in the cultural conflicts between democratic choices and an open society on the one hand and closed, authoritarian societies on the other. Karl Popper famously made a distinction between 'The Open Society and its Enemies', linking economic organisation to fundamental values; but today (and really it was always so) fundamental values are directly on the front line in political and economic struggles against authoritarianism. The Maidan Museum has special significance in Ukraine itself, but it has a much wider global significance. While it could be said that it has a particular resonance in Europe, the conflicts of values and social practices at issue are equally in question in Myanmar, in much of Hispanic America, in every part of Africa where a struggle for a free society and an uncorrupted democracy is unresolved, and even in that supposed bastion of democratic ideals the United States, particularly in the aftermath of the assault to overturn democracy there on 6 January 2021. That remains no less true even though in his book, Giovanni Ercolani has tried in careful forensic analysis to explore the meanings and language and emotional weight of the Museum without political rhetoric. He brings the discipline of anthropology to bear on the representations of those conflicts. The point is that the anthropological gaze leads to a sharper understanding of those wider issues, as well as to a deeper understanding of the practices, symbolism, spiritual resonances and social communication which the Museum offers. This foreword will also suggest a sense in which memory, history, memorialisation and the creation of art carry a particular weight in the constructions of identities (the plurals are important).

But first, what, more precisely, is the Maidan Museum about? From its name, many people might expect the museum to be a building, probably rather stolid, in the centre of a major town, with a particular organisation around given themes, often chronological, with a story or series of stories to tell- but above all a location, a place, devoted to memory and identity. The major museums and galleries in any great city -the Prado in Madrid, the British Museum or Museum of Childhood in London, the great museums of antiquities and national heritage in Cairo, Baghdad and Saskatchewan in Canada- all follow similar models. The Maidan Museum at once conforms and deviates from this. First of all, the museum currently does not have a permanent home. It is partly housed temporarily before a planned large-scale building is completed, a dramatic design which, when completed, would be one of the premier European museums to rank with the two Gugenheims in Bilbao and Lisbon, Daniel Libeskind's Berlin Jewish Museum, and Zaha Haddid's Riverside Museum in Glasgow. The plans for a new radical building, yet to be built, have been delayed both by internal arguments, by disputes over funding, and by the coming of war. But the museum as it exists lives on the streets, and in Maidan Square. It is also an outreach project, taken by enthusiasts to schools, regional museums and community centres across Ukraine. It is, more than anything else, a spirit which commemorates the spirit of the events of 2012/13, an attempt, if you like, at keeping alight a flame of permanent democratic revolution. Ercolani explains the significance of this more fully in his Chapter Five.

The optimism apparent in the project of Maidan defies some current realities: it asserts an optimistic vision of the future. Above all, Maidan is different from most 'museums', including those mentioned above, because it has been made by the people it wants to remember, commemorate, celebrate. Like the Holocaust Museums in Washington DC and Berlin, it remembers the dead; but it also remembers the actions and courage of the living. And it perpetuates what its founders would say was 'Ukraine at its best'. That Ukraine stands in defiance of forces of corruption and coercive domination, as much by western capital or corporate power, as by Russian oligarchy and Putinesque nationalism. The fact that the Museum was created by people directly involved in the events whose spirit it conjures gives it a unique character. They also endow it with a diversity of meanings, a spiritual and profane weight, which is pretty much unique in any major national museum in a capital city. It is that diversity of meanings, that collision of spiritual, political and historic power, which Ercolani aims to unravel and explore. Because it is a spirit as much as a material thing, an ongoing practice as much as a presentation of the past, it is especially appropriate to use the anthropological approach of this study. As he does so, he takes the position of a stranger in a new territory which, although not wholly unfamiliar, demands a fresh eye and new ways of evaluation. What especially characterises that approach is the ways it privileges the ideas and beliefs and language and social practices of those who create it, and who continue to build its evolving meanings and significance. That understanding is based on a series of interviews, mostly in considerable depth, with key participants in the making of Maidan. Ritual, symbolism, what is sacred and what is made sacred engage together in the practices of the Museum in ways which are life-affirming and identity-creating for the people of Ukraine. The wider importance lies in the importance of an effort to practice bottom-up popular democracy in defiance of both moneyed oligarchy and authoritarian violence. It overlaps with, but is separate and complementary to, a purely aesthetic approach or a merely political analysis of the Museum.

In their attack on Ukraine from 24 February 2022, Russian forces have systematically destroyed sites and emblems of any distinctive identity, including over 200 museums and memorials, many public buildings, and not a few churches. The cultural goals of the invasion include, but are not limited to, wiping out any history of Ukraine which denies that the country has always been in substantial measure subservient to Moscow. That project is already being actively pursued in schools that have fallen under the control of Russia's military. New textbooks have been imposed which reflect Putin's personal view of the history of Russia-Ukraine relations. His view is that Peter the Great did Ukraine a favour in re-integrating it into 'Greater Russia' that previously had mythic existence before the Russia-Ukraine connection was destroyed by the Mongol invasions of the thirteenth century and the Polish invasions of the fifteenth. As already noted, this is not a historical account shared in most of Ukraine. This cultural warfare reflects a myth promoted by Tsarist governments after they conquered major parts of Ukraine in the early eighteenth century. It was sustained by the Bolshevik governments after 1917, when for a short time Ukraine became a wholly independent state, separate from Moscow, under a partly anarchist government. Bolshevik policies from 1924 onwards were reinforced by racial and ethnic policies which tried as far as possible to eliminate whole groups in Ukraine, such as the German (Saxon) settlements dating back to the thirteenth century, the. Crimean Tartar people, as well as Cossack and other communities. Western Ukraine is close culturally and historically to Poland; south western Ukraine has people with Romanian and Hungarian heritage. There are, of course, also substantial Russian communities across Ukraine, and especially in the east, but they are part of a multicultural mix with a complex, deep-rooted history. Although Russian missiles have not (so far) directly targeted the Maidan commemorations, and would find it hard to do so, given that they are so diffused, so much based in outreach and online expressions, the Russian army would undoubtedly destroy Maidan as a space and as a spirit if they could.

The Ukrainian Orthodox church had been partially autonomous from the Moscow Metropolitan for many years. But, under personal encouragement from President Putin, the Moscow church has sought to re-establish closer control over Kyiv's orthodox community, a complicated theological story which led eventually to the Ukrainian Orthodox church declaring full autonomy from Moscow in 2018. One of the aims of the invasion in quite certainly to restore Moscow's complete religious control, and to kill or at least imprison priests and religious thinkers who defend the separateness of the two religilous communities. Although quite a good number of Ukrainian citizens are not personally religious, Ukrainian national spirit could not be corralled by Moscow without destroying Kyiv's distinctive church -which is in fact far older than that in Moscow. In the analysis which Ercolani offers of the Maidan Museum and the 'Spirit of Maidan', he gives a much fuller account of the sacred nature of the lives the Museum commemorates and the artefacts which it uses to embody a range of human experiences. He contends that there are processes of sacralization in the act of making the Museum, but also in the very ways in which one might visit and seek to understand its objects and artefacts, including music and poetry as well as art work and sculpture as well as 'found objects' from the conflicts on the streets.

Contending Histories and Memories

One of the roles of the Maidan Museum is, therefore, to hold and protect memories of recent events and the people who made them, suffered for them, and in some cases, around one hundred individuals, died. They memorialize the present, not some distant past, and they do so in order to suspend time and keep those events and people in the present. Anthropology recognizes that it is quite common, perhaps even indispensable, for peoples to engage in rituals and practices which suspend time and create meanings out of those actions. And here it is important to add that while in the not so distant past, anthropology was a part of a colonial enterprise which purported to study a 'primitive other', as a subject it has battled that stereotype (perhaps that battle continues, but that is not the issue here). At the same time, anthropologists have turned their attention to the societies immediately around them, to the self-understandings of Japanese business executives, to European football ultras, to the daily lives of prisoners, to women's shared experience of menopause, and to the rituals of teenage fandom (to cite just a few examples). Where communities in the global south are studied, the methods assumptions and language are certainly very different from the 1920s and 1930s, when anthropology established itself in the academy.

Earlier, I compared the Maidan Museum in some important respects to the various Holocaust museums which have been created, mostly only in the last thirty years: the Washington Museum opened in 1994; the Jewish Museum in Berlin in 2001; only Yad Vashem was opened earlier in Jerusalem, in 1953. The comparison is apt in several ways. Each of these institutions raises questions about how the past can be represented, and who can do so. The answer to those questions in each of those cases is that this particular past cannot be 'represented' and perhaps must not be: it can only be *presented*: as Emmanuel Levinas argued, it can be shown, and born witness to, but not 're-presented' without distortion and dishonesty. It helps that there is testimony from survivors, and there are many such testimonies, but much of the weight of the Holocaust memorials lies in a simple showing of evidence - family letters, photographs, short film clips, piles of shoes or hair or toys left along a trip to the crematorium. Through this evidence, the museum curators try to reach out to the visitor and give them an experience in which they (the curators) seem to have mediated as little as possible, to let those people speak directly to each of us. Visiting the Washington Museum in 1994, I was asked from first entering to carry a card showing the name and age of an individual woman who died in Theresienstadt to root my experience witnessing a whole body of physical evidence, narratives, images and film, History with a capital 'H', an overwhelming two hours emotional and factual bombardment, related in this way to the life and death of a single, recognizable named human being. I still have it on my desk. Maidan makes that connection between individuals; at the same time, it *presents* the 'big History' through the evidence of individuals who took part in events, through the use of personal memorials from children or family, photographs and clips (now recorded on phones and tablets), as well as personal biographies. And it invites visitors to make their own interpretations and conclusions.

There is a kind of sentimentality here, but in saying it is a kind of sentimentality, I do not mean anything cheap or unimportant. Philosophy, feminist thinking, theatre and a great deal more remind us of the importance of emotion alongside other human reasoning and human passions. Even in the supposed 'rationalist' business of academic economics, recent work, including that of at least two Nobel prize winners, emphasizes the importance of emotion alongside calculation in economic decision making. How we integrate an understanding of our own emotions and reactions to events which are a great burden, even if they are not as overwhelming as the Holocaust, is an important question for anyone who tries to understand the recent past and to memorialize histories we have lived through. This integration of emotion and reasoned argument was clearly important for the founders of the Maidan Museum. Interrogating it is a theme which runs through much of Giovanni Ercolani's work, noting that emotional responses to the Museum are very important just so long as the visitor -or here the reader- does not allow their responses to be reduced to emotion alone. The evidence of Ercolani's various witnesses and interviewees demonstrates how central this is to the experience of Maidan. What the book shows is how an account can sensitively draw together a reasoned account of myths, rituals and passionate emotions in the creation of a world of life and identity understood through the sacrifice of others.

Recognizing Russians and the West in All This

The current government is Moscow initially set about what it called a 'special military operation' claiming it was 'liberating' parts of Ukraine from 'Nazis', seeming to mean the present parties in power. Since the invasion began in February 2022, it has imprisoned thousands of its own people for protesting against the war, some merely for calling it a 'war' rather than the required public vocabulary of 'special military operation'. But as the conflict unfolded, Russian intentions have become more sweeping -to 'liberate' all of Ukraine, to define all Ukrainian nationalism as 'Nazi' and so to eliminate the spirit and identity of the people. After months of unsuccessful warfare, Putin's agents now point more to the west as having 'occupied' Ukraine as a justification for their invasion. As in many wars, the war aims shifted, not necessarily under the full control of the protagonists. By 'Nazi', Putin and his acolytes appear now to mean (nonsensically) anyone with a sense of the distinctive identity of Ukraine and Ukrainians. Yet many people who identify as ethnic Russians and Russian speakers living in Ukraine have joined the war of resistance against the invasion, and Putin has only succeeded in unifying the country more than any other action might have done. Putin has compared himself to the Tsar Peter the Great, who conquered large parts of the Polish/Lithuanian Commonwealth as well as largely destroying the previously dominant Swedish Empire in the Great Northern War (1700-1721), including much of modern Ukraine. The culminating battle of that war was fought at Poltava, now in Ukraine between Kyiv and the Russian city of Belgorod. Peter succeeded in destroying a republican and partially democratic system of government which had linked Poland, Lithuania, Ukraine and parts of what are now the Baltic states for nearly four hundred years, and which give Ukraine longstanding links to Europe rather than to Russia. Those links have never disappeared, especially among the largely catholic population of western Ukraine. But the events of 2013-4 were a powerful drive towards reorienting all of Ukraine more towards the European Union and the west and away from both Russia and the Soviet past. After heavy losses and grave international embarrassments, Putin's aims seem to have extended to the extinction of Ukrainian independence. I say 'seems to have' because Putin has mostly tried to couch his actual aims in such woolly terms, probably so that he could claim victory pretty much whatever the final outcome of the war might be. But it does not seem mistaken to conclude that we know from actions on the battlefield, from their treatment of civilians, from their forced deportation of tens of thousands of people, that Russian ambitions are to extinguish a distinctive identity as well as a sovereign nation. That this breaks international law and a whole raft of treaties to which the Russian Federation has acceded does not matter to Putin, who has declared more than once that his underlying aim is also to re-shape the post Cold War international order in a manner of his choosing. The Museum might be taken to represent a 'special cultural operation' in defiance of Putin's 'special military operation', and this articulation of a counter to remnants of soviet culture as well as to Putin's imperial project is developed much more fully, especially by some of the key interviewees in the book.

But it is important, I think, to make three comments about Putin's view of the world. First of all, not all Russian people share it, and many Russian people, especially those with close family or other ties to Ukraine, will be deeply opposed to it, even if they have been terrified into silence by the apparatus of the Russian state. Nothing in Ercolani's book, or in this Foreword, should be taken to suggest a crude binary opposition between Russia and Ukraine, and that is not the main thrust of the Museum's exhibits and spirit either. Many other Russian people are victims of state violence for other reasons, many others might see themselves more as entitled to western levels of human rights and dignity, not to mention the higher standards of living which European Union member countries enjoy. The limited media coverage of Russian society suggests that the government has worked very hard to suppress any organization among mothers of war casualties, who were one of the most powerful opponents of the (much more limited) Russian war in Afghanistan, but which played a key role in the eventual collapse of the Soviet Union in 1991 after the Afghan defeat. But most Russians clearly support their government because they have no choice, because they are victims of a corrupted media, because they are bombarded with propaganda and have been for a generation, and because they have no access to alternative media whether online or broadcast which might challenge the monolith of Moscow-speak. And those people too are victims, although they themselves might not accept that description right now.

The second thing it is important to say about Putin's view of the world is that it is, in a limited sense, correct. It is not 'right' -this is not a justification for the violence of the attack on Ukraine. But Russian leaders were promised that NATO would not expand (a promise that perhaps should not have been given). They were, or seem to have been, promised that East Germany would not be absorbed into NATO when it was merged with the former West Germany (a dishonest promise from the start that quite certainly should not have been made). They were also promised a much greater deal of consultation through post Cold War diplomatic machinery than became the actual practice: the leading EU and G7 governments basked in what was foolishly seen as a 'triumph of the west' in the 1990s, while the losers could be relegated to a second division of global players. Again, this does not justify current Russian aggression. But it is a key element in the current conflict, as western government officials understand very well. Russia's status as a great power diplomatically was relegated as much as its military capability or economic strengths. Putin came to power in 2000 resolved to overturn this state of affairs and has consistently followed through on his ambition to restore Russian standing. However disgusting his behaviour, this is a part of his project, which appears to be popular in the eyes of many, but not all, Russians.

The third point I would make about the present conflict is that from 1992 to February 2022, Ukraine had been caught in an economic struggle which was as harmful as it was self-interested. That self-interest was commercial and financial. Western financial interests vied with Russian oligarchs and others to seize Ukraine's assets, to entrench Ukrainian indebtedness, to take over companies and control the minerals and agricultural strengths on which much of the country's economy is grounded. This is a murky story, but it is beyond dispute that Ukraine was scarred by corruption which threatened to undermine what popular democracy was possible, and which was characterized also by struggles for media ownership. Some western interests were heavily involved in these conflicts, which included grabs for mineral and agricultural resources as well as for control of the banking system. This was a contested field which led to the rise of now President Zelensky: Zelensky was elected in large part to try to move the country more towards EU membership by a popular movement which was rightly suspicious of the levels of corporate power and corruption in Ukraine. And the 'Spirit of Maidan' has sought to challenge this western subversion of democracy as it has sought to overturn Russian leverage and the remnants of soviet thinking. Again, none of this justifies the Russian invasion. The radical democrats who wanted to change the government in 2013-14 were as conscious of the level of corruption as they were of the threat of Russian military power, and that is explicit in many of the memorials in the Museum. Maidan is thus intended to represent the better parts of the Ukrainian people, and it takes a stand as much against the corporate corruption of the previous twenty years as against specific politicians and political cabals. This is an assertion of a popular imagination of a better world in which citizens in many would-be democracies that are blighted by corrupt media ownership and behind-the-scenes corporate manipulation can respect. For the Maidan Museum does not reflect what Ukraine is today so much as what Ukrainians would wish all democratic countries to be, an example to learn from even in much older so-called democracies.

The Aesthetics of Maidan

Ercolani is explicit that his is a study the practice of an aesthetics using anthropology as the means of exploration. That is, the Maidan Museum creates objects of beauty, experiences which inspire awe and dread, which provoke judgment and debate, which challenge the senses and one's judgment. This is to talk of aesthetics in a contemporary sense. It does not necessarily refer to any 'classical' model of 'beauty' where the object is the creation of a sense of a contested 'sublime' of the form advanced especially in 1757 by Edmund Gibbon (1998), as well as by Kant and the eighteenth-century enlightenment. In the contemporary argument, beauty is neither static nor fixed in a formula, although it can be taught and shared. But its quality may lie in its elusiveness, in fluidity, and in the ways in which each authorial voice (in Maidan a collective as well as a series of individuals) makes their own aesthetics. As the musicians Pussy Riot showed in their various performances, this can be equally a political and an aesthetic path. Jacques Rancière (2014) has compared the importance of the conversations which take place between the political and the aesthetic, 'emplotments of autonomy and heteronomy' (p.115). Maidan is very obviously a deliberate political provocation as well as a record of experience in which the viewer/visitor is invited to join. Rancière continues: 'the autonomy is the autonomy of the experience, not of the work of art. In other words, the artwork participates in the sensorium of autonomy inasmuch as it is not a work of art' (p.117). In this sense it is not what the artist or author or photographer intends to say but what the viewer or listener or participant in a performance experience which has priority in interpreting artwork which is always, whatever else, both political and personal. This poses a problem of problem of democracy and democratization of meaning: meanings are created, and dismantled, by viewers and listeners and readers, but how that happens and how that is controlled is in itself an important political question. That Maidan is created by those whose experience it narrates and contextualizes is of special importance.

Drawing on Rancière's discussion of the relationship between politics and art helps to make sense of the diversity of the objects and representations in the Maidan Museum, some of which are entirely personal, some addressed to a son or brother or father, some more ambitious in intended audience, but not first of all intended as 'public art', whereas others look outward to embrace the wider public of the city and the community of viewers and visitors.

An Anthropological Gaze

There are obvious and important political questions, including fundamental problems in European political theory, in the untangling of the significance of Maidan -the museum and the events of 2012/13 as well as its changed meanings today. What Ercolani's anthropological gaze turns to are the rituals and practices which underpin the 'performance' of Maidan, or the memorialization of the events of 2013-14, and of their changing meanings in the present to those who created the Museum and those who take part in it either in personal visits or online experience. He borrows the language of aesthetics and aestheticization –how an object or practice which might not at first resonate as an art object or practice becomes invested with an aesthetic value- from a contemporary literature, including Rancière. He treats the notion of myth as central to the purpose of the Museum, and brings the important recent work of the Canadian scholar Gerard Bouchard (2017) on myths and social rituals to bear to understand more fully what the importance of Maidan is. In doing so, he also extends some key ideas in recent social anthropology. To a non-anthropologist reader, this may seem quaint: when I was growing up, to say that what another boy said was a myth was a slightly polite way of saying he was lying. But myths are not lies, and if they embody deliberate untruths they are unlikely to survive for very long. Rather, myths are non-literal truths. They are stories which capture a reality of lived experience for the communities which share them. They have power because they offer a kind of explanation which is consistent with other ways in which the world is understood, whether they are about the creation of the world, a people's relations with the natural environment or how one faces basic problems of life, death, morality and possible societal collapse. This is as much the case with classic myths such as the Greek narratives of the gods or the earliest known epic, The Story of Gilgamesh, as it is of contemporary myths and mythologizing. They encompass much of what the philosopher Wittgenstein calls 'a form of life', a way of living within and in relation to a specific language.

Maidan does not *create* the mythology of Ukrainian independence, but it sustains and elaborates it, and it creates a language within which the sacrifice of individuals' lives becomes intelligible and praiseworthy. At the same time, it carries the set of meanings over to a wider sense. Again, the Museum does not *create* the modern sense of national identity, which derives primarily from folklorists, historians, politicians and writers in the nineteenth century, as it does for most other European countries. Rather, it deepens and defines that sense of identity in the particular context of the twenty-first century. That engages with a kind of religious or at least spiritual power: what is sacred, what can be spoken of, what is true within the rituals and social exchanges of Maidan, in the memorialization of painful and joyful shared events. Ercolani's main aim, drawing importantly on Bouchard's (2011) work (among others) is to show how that sense of the sacred intertwines with the myths and memories in order to form a broadly coherent whole on which national identity can be grounded, but on which, at the same time, individuals and families can find meaning as they grieve and celebrate.

Translations

Any discussion of the significance of a museum such as Maidan requires a number of stages of translation. Most obviously, we translate from natural languages -English, Russian, Ukrainian, Polish, French and so on. But we also translate from the distinctiveness of what, as I noted already, Ludwig Wittgenstein called 'forms of life', ways of being and relating to each other which give the essentially social and shared character of language its force and meanings. What the individuals who fought and sometimes died for in the independence struggles in Czech, Polish, Romanian or Ukrainian contexts have a lot in common; but in each case it is also different, distinctive. One 'velvet revolution' is not the same as any other, and some have little of the smoothness of velvet about them. Some linguistic theorists might suggest that we cannot translate the experience, feelings and meanings of one struggle to another, just as we cannot translate the untranslatable depth of meaning in poetry. I beg to differ. First, one might present the great translations of Seamus Heaney or Simon Armitage, or the extraordinary achievement of Edith Hall's translations of classic Greek drama. Disputes about translation also revolve around the translation of Paul Celan's poetry or the writing of Ingeborg Bachmann or Nelly Sachs. Different and more difficult questions arise translating classical or modern Chinese and Japanese literature. But great translations of these European poets work exist. This quickly leads to a second argument. Heaney, Armitage and Hall have all written extensively about their understanding of translation, and each emphasizes their agreement that they *cannot fully* translate the exact meanings - denotations and connotations, metaphor and force of symbolic meaning- of the words they deploy. The translator chooses the words and rhythms they use to capture what they think is critical to an understanding; but they know that just as a contemporary reading of Beowulf, Pearl or Antigone in the original language will not mean the same to a contemporary audience, however linguistically gifted, as they did to their original audiences, so the translation will lose something. Another translation, another story, is always possible. But at the same time, it will gain something, and in the hands of a gifted writer, especially one as gifted as any of these three examples, a text becomes reanimated, acquires new meanings and relates to contemporary sensibilities and priorities, even if it inevitably loses others in the process. So translating is itself an act of creation, although it must also be as precise as possible to stand as a valid piece of work.

The reason why this argument about translation is important here is because actually we engage in translation all the time in everyday life. We may not be as great a writer as Heaney or as powerful a scholar as Hall, but when we talk to others we reach out to them across barriers of different experience and different expectations. Every conversation is in this sense a translation, even between users of the same natural language. But even within the same natural language, we often do not speak in the same register, and each register reflects a distinctive form of life: for example, in lecturing I might use one register, in speaking to my mother another, and in standing on the football terraces I might use quite a different mode of speech: the routine obscenities of football or the parade ground would get me fired if I used them in class, and deeply condemned if speaking to my mother. Each person uses different languages and different modes of address all the time, unless, they live in a single capsule. As an aging academic, I have to make sure I understand the language used by nineteen year old students, much of which would have been as foreign to my nineteen year old self as Spanish or Italian (languages of which I have a thin, but only a thin, grasp). So the Maidan Museum reflects distinctive experiences, struggles, anxieties, deaths, threats and triumphs of which most people reading this book will only be dimly aware. My point is that everything we engage in socially involves translation, and yet that translation is, with good will and careful attention to the other person, possible, albeit not perfectly. This argument that social exchange is a dialogue is elaborated more technically in Farrands, 2000 (see also Moore and Farrands, 2012 and Ricoeur, 1992). Translation is a dialogue; sense making, the core practice of anthropology and of all of the humanities, is dialogic. It is not just the responsibility of the speaker to make herself plain. It is equally the listener who reaches out to her. It is through the dialogue of exchange, not through the 'purity' of speech or intentions of the speaker or the listener's knowledge and skill, that translations are achieved. And although he never makes that claim, what Ercolani does is to show us more clearly how we can make sense of the experience of those who established the Maidan Museum and those who maintain its flame even in the face of war. He enters a dialogue, an archaeology of Maidan in the present. It is quite an achievement, although he would be the first to say it is imperfect. But like all translation, that is unavoidable.

Fluidities and Fixtures

Throughout his study, Ercolani refers to 'Maidanization'. By that he means the process of establishing a mythology that holds as a central truth the messages of both the past and the present conflicts as central to Ukrainian identity. But it is also a mythology that establishes Ukrainian experience as central to European identity. That is to say that the Museum and the spirit it represents is about much more than a desire on the part of many most? Ukrainians to join the European Union. It is more an assertion of the continuity of a sense that Ukraine has always been much more part of Europe than the counter myth that it is part of Russia would argue. This is not straightforward. I am sure I would not be alone in thinking that Russia itself is, for all the political divisions which have existed from time to time, also a part of Europe. That may be a 'fact' geographically for the western part of Russia. But I mean much more that, intellectually and historically, Russia is European: try to imagine the trajectory of European music without Tchaikovsky or Stravinsky, the European novel without Tolstoy and Bulgakov, poetry without Akhmatova and Pushkin, or history without Russia's roles in the Napoleonic wars and World War Two. Equally, all these distinctively Russian voices owe something to European predecessors. And Russian anarchism owes a great deal to France, while Marxism, although dissimilar in many respects from what turned out to be Russian communism, was conceived in Germany and Britain. Russian industrialization after 1921 followed the model set by Henry Ford as often as it did anything written in the dank, derivative theories of Lenin and his colleagues. Russian capitalism after 1991 derives from an imposed western, mainly US, model, and not a small share of Russia's technology was bought or stolen from the west. One could go on, but for the moment I rest the case that Russia is also in significant ways, not all of them pretty, closely linked to Europe and the 'West'. Museums fix something - in both senses. They create and then try to cement a vision of reality, the spirit which holds an identity through a narrative of the past. At the same time, they try to fix a problem, to engineer a solution of a kind, even if the 'problem' they identify is not one which many people outside the curation team would see as an issue, a doubt about identity, memory and story. The Maidan Museum was designed to do much of this, but also to recognize that Ukrainian identities, histories and memories are fractured and fluid, contested, and yet have sufficient common grounds to draw a people together.

How can a changing memorial be curated? Whatever we think the Maidan Museum is about, its significance has changed because of the war, because of the unexpected strength and effectiveness of Ukrainian resistance, because the war has in some senses been a global struggle, but also because of the changing political and cultural questions at issue indirectly as a consequence of the conflict. During the course of his discussion, Ercolani interviews a number of people who have been or who still are engaged directly in that question. How the Museum stays alive and relevant, how it discharges the responsibilities it has taken on, remain active questions with which key interviewees engage. This in turn invites the reader to do more than draw their own conclusions, but also to ask themselves what wider responsibilities and engagements they might take away from their encounter with the Museum. Here, Ercolani is careful: he does not make any attempt to tell the reader how they should respond to his arguments and to his exposure of the importance of the spirit of Maidan/EuroMaidan. But his account does make it clear one can hardly remain indifferent with the experience of that spirit. It is then up to the reader to decide what to do with their answers to the question posed.

I hope this Foreword has been fair to the text it introduces, but I can hardly claim I am a disinterested observer. I should admit that I have known Giovanni Ercolani as a scholar and as a friend for a good length of time. I was honoured that he invited me to read the original text on which this book is based and then to write this Foreword for this publication. The book speaks for itself, and will be of great interest to academic anthropology because of its subject and also because of its innovative thinking, language and methods. But it will also be much more widely interesting to anyone who takes seriously the relationships between art, politics and social practice; it will be equally significant for anyone engaged in the various debates about memorialization, responsibility and the re/presentation of the past, a substantial debate among recent social historians. It will capture the attention of those interested in museum practice and the curating of the recent past. It will twinkle the interest of anyone drawn to debates about the sacred and the patterns of symbolism and language in sacralization in secular society, sociologist or theologian. It will be of lasting significance, whatever the outcome of the current conflict, for anyone interested not just in the future of Ukraine, but also the future of Europe. It may be quite a short study, but it is all the same a significant one.

Chris Farrands, PhD, FRSA, FRAI
Nottingham Trent University
July 27th, 2022

Preface

As a sociocultural anthropologist, in 2016, I developed an interest in the relationship between art, identity, and the Maidan events. The same year I travelled to Kyiv to collect materials on this topic in the course of which, in November, I met Dr Ihor Poshyvailo, Director of the Maidan Museum, in the offices of the Ivan Honchar Museum, where he then was the Deputy Director. At that moment, the Maidan Museum was an ambitious project, a difficult work in progress, strongly opposed by political powers. Dr Poshyvailo showed me a store full of boxes containing materials and works of art he had been collecting with his small team from Maidan and which constituted ban embryonic basis for the collections of a future museum envisioned by a group of museum professionals and public activists.

I was won over by the enthusiasm of Dr Poshyvailo and the idea to focus my research on the 'establishment' of the Maidan Museum appealed to me. During the years I met again Dr Poshyvailo in Rome (Italy) and in Kyiv, where I was offered an internship at the National Memorial of the Heavenly Hundred Heroes and Revolution of Dignity Museum.

During my internship I came in contact with my informants: members of the Maidan Museum, artists who participated at the Maidan events and inspired by Revolution of Dignity produced 'art', historians, and shaped the Spirit of Maidan. I was there, I spent time with them, I talked to them, I interviewed them, I listened to them, they shared with me their strong emotions and dramatic memories of the Maidan, and I suffered with them. I collected fourteen interviews, photographic material—I am responsible for the majority of the photos in this text—and I observed the deep human feelings still lasting in some of the people, including artists, with whom I came in contact.

At the end of my internship I gave a public lecture at the Information and Exhibition Center of the Maidan Museum on 'Art, Identity, and Security: the Case of the Maidan Museum'. This text presents the results of my research project.

1
The Maidan Museum: Art and Identity

1.1 Introduction

The National Memorial of the Heavenly Hundred Heroes and Revolution of Dignity Museum, in the following the Maidan Musem, is a work-in-progress museum in Kyiv, Ukraine. The museum preserves narratives, documentation, objects and works of arts left, produced, and inspired by the Revolution of Dignity (November 21, 2013 – February 23, 2014) which took place in Independence Square (nicknamed Maidan) in Kyiv and in many other cities and regions throughout Ukraine, as well as many cities of the world with strong Ukrainian diaspora populations. In the following, the terms 'Maidan Events', 'Euromaidan', and 'the Revolution of Dignity' are used interchangeably.

The Maidan Museum is the only national museum devoted to commemorating, collecting, exhibiting, interpreting and disseminating the narratives of the struggle by Ukrainians for national independence, human rights, individual freedoms, dignity, identity, and more importantly, to preserve the Spirit of Maidan. The language and narrative produced by the Maidan Museum is communicated through the use of the works of arts of the Euromaidan Revolution ('the Maidan'), demonstrating in this way the strong connection between art and political-identitarian discourse. The term 'Euromaidan' captures the desire of those who made that revolution to assert a European identity and a place in European history; it is not merely an expression of a wish which many of its proponents share that Ukraine should join the European Union.

The academic methodology adopted in this theoretical research of a core concept grows from that of Fine Arts research, in which the concept and the context of art production is investigated. This means that the 'research is aimed at the practices of artistic creation and their visual products, as well as the contexts in which it takes place, and has an eminently theoretical character' (Galindo

Mateo and Martin Martinez, 2007: 56). It is based on field work and its purpose is to analyze the role of the Museum of Maidan as a memorial of the Euromaidan Revolution (or Revolution of Dignity, 2013-2014) and the Spirit of Maidan.

The research therefore establishes 'the Maidan' ('Euromaidan Revolution') as the central concept and context of this work. It examines the Maidan Museum's political discourse of resistance, civil disobedience and solidarity as produced through artistic activities-performances-exhibitions-rituals. It considers the contribution the Maidan Museum's activities make to the gestation of a post-Maidan Ukrainian identity based on the Spirit of Maidan. It suggests that Ukrainian national memory, culture, awareness and consciousness activated and originated during the Euromaidan events; and circumscribes and it presents the concept of the 'Maidanization process'.

What is more, 'what the Maidan-Euromaidan-Revolution of Dignity stands for is, first and foremost, a value-based vision of Ukraine as part of a wider Europe. It is adherence to a set of values born at the dawn of European modernity that could — and should — become a cornerstone of the overarching Ukrainian national identity. To be sure, what is truly important about these values — rule of law, division between public and private spheres, human rights, freedom — is not so much that they are European (although, historically, they are) as that they are universal. They appeal equally, and irrespective of concrete cultural context, to a Frenchman, an Ukrainian, and a Russian' (Torbakov, 2018: 197).

The Maidan Museum is grounded on the events and the message of the Revolution of Dignity. This was a revolution for national values and identity and it was a bloody identity struggle, in which art played an important role because it narrated, visualized, and symbolized the struggle and its roots, shaped the Spirit of Maidan, and identified the main features (defined here as the symbols of Maidan) of the post-Euromaidan Ukrainian identity (Moussienko, 2016). The concept of the Maidan represents the social and symbolic capital, in a bourdieusian sense (Bourdieu, 2005), of the Maidan Museum.

Euromaidan or Revolution of Dignity (November 21, 2013 – February 23, 2014) refers to a series of mass protests against the government of the then president, Víktor Yanukovych, by various groups in favor of the signing of the long-negotiated Association Agreement and the Free Trade Agreement with the European Union, contrary to an agreement with the Russian Federation. The protests were started mostly by journalists and university students. However, different sectors of the population joined subsequently, all dissatisfied with the management of the governing Party of the Regions and the results of its socio-economic and geopolitical policies. It is notable that there were no one formal organizer of the movement: it was coordinated by various public initiatives, which all declared not to be associated with any political party. Among the main actors of the protests were: NGOs, social organizations, the political opposition – including the far-right nationalist group Pravyi Sektor, one of the most active of the movement in Kyiv, and the far-right parliamentary party Svoboda, as well as the Ukrainian Churches – such as the Ukrainian Greek Catholic Church and the Ukrainian Orthodox Church of the Kyiv Patriarchate – with the exception of the Ukrainian Orthodox Church of the Moscow Patriarchate. Representatives of ethnic minorities – Russians, Crimean Tatars, Jews, Georgians, Armenians and others – and citizens of other countries (from Poland, Belarus, Georgia, Russia, EU, USA and others) also participated in the demonstrations. They were joined by some philosophical groups and by opponents in general of the political and economic management of the Ukrainian political elite, who they accused of corruption and illicit enrichment. Held mainly in the western and central parts of the country but also to some degree the southern and eastern regions – now occupied Donetsk, Luhansk and Crimea. The center of the protests was the Independence Square (Maidán Nezalézhnosti in Ukrainian) in Kyiv, from which the name of the movement originates. During January 2014, European protests continued, with protesters making increasingly widespread use of means of protection such as professional, improvised helmets, vests and even riot shields. The protests led to riots. These also grew in intensity to the point that there were days, when many protesters continued their protests throughout the night, making it impossible for the authorities to evict them from the place.

On January 16, the Rada issued a law considered by many to be anti-democratic, the provisions of which established penalties against protesters, as well as against the blockade of administrative buildings and the installation of tents. This was perceived by the protesters as a veto of their right to demonstrate and protest and thus as a reduction of their human rights and freedoms. That crucial moment caused a considerable escalation of violence in an attempt to cause the rejection of the new laws passed by government. As a result, on January 22, the demonstrations witnessed five deaths for the first time since their beginning. On the night of February 19-20, the Ukrainian government and the opposition agreed to a truce that the leader of the main opposition party described as 'good news'. After six hours in force, the truce was broken and riots broke out again. This time firearms were used by the riot police. Some media reported that twenty-one protesters were shot dead the morning after the truce and called the climate in Kyiv 'pre-civil war'. The Interior Minister, Vitaliy Zajárchenko, ordered the issuance of combat weapons to the police that same afternoon and described the mission of the law enforcement personnel as an 'anti-terrorist operation'. Also in that same afternoon, medical sources close to the opposition put the death toll at around one hundred, while official sources kept it at sixty-seven. The opponents were holding sixty-seven police officers captured that time. While the opposition claimed in a statement that the police had been ordered to 'shoot to kill', the Government declared that its forces were acting 'in legitimate defense' against opposition violence.

February 20 ('Black Thursday') was considered the most violent day of the riots, with more than sixty deaths, mainly around the Kyiv Independence Square (Maidan), the heart of the protests. Shocking images went around the world through the Internet and social networks. Finally, on February 21, an agreement was approved between Yanukovych and the opposition to bring forward elections, form a transitional government, return to the 2004 Constitution, and stop the violence. The same day Yanukovych fled from his residency near Kyiv to Kharkiv and then to Russia. On February 22, the Ukrainian Parliament (Rada) declared the removal of Viktor Yanukovych from office as President of Ukraine and called new presidential elections for May.

Figure 1. Mural in Kyiv. (Photo credit: G. Ercolani, 2019)

As demonstrated by the work of Moussienko (2016), dedicated to the art of Maidan, during the Euromaidan events hundreds of artists—both professionals and amateurs—openly expressed their strong feelings and emotions, and communicated their attitudes towards what was going on around them. Through the production of meaningful art, they questioned stereotypes and conventions and explored the characteristics that determine their personal and social identity. They constructed a consciousness and a sense of 'who we are' as individuals, as a society, and as a nation. And they actively became involved in 'artivism' (Milohnic, 2005), and as engaged and committed artists created visual identities. They engaged protesters and the Maidan territory visitors into artistic expressions in physical spaces of protest worldwide, as well as on social media. Painters, dancers, musicians, performers, illustrators as well as ordinary people created poems, novels, songs and music, painted helmets and shields, designed funny posters and humorous installations, decorated barricades, cars, tents, trees, streets and buildings, organized flash mobs, performances, concerts and exhibitions. Together they formed the Artistic Squadron and Union of Artists of Maidan. Basically 'the art of Maidan covered the road from carnival to sacral and organically combined in itself elements of avant-garde, mass culture, and high classicism that is characteristic of our era of the post modern' (Moussienko, 2016: 7). It is therefore clear that the art of Maidan embodies the symbols of identity, the emotions, the energy, the hope, the expectations and the dreams of the Post-Maidan Ukrainian identity. It also, as figure 1 eloquently testifies, looks towards a future which is European, at least in the sense of embracing free speech, democracy and the rule of law, and the core values of what Ukrainians often see, perhaps sometimes over-idealistically, as the values of the European Union.

In Maidan, creativity erupted in its explosive and contagious dimension. So long forgotten and repressed during the Soviet Union time, this unchained creativity gave shape to its opus which is the Maidan, and with it the spirit, the soul of Maidan. For James Hillman, who has studied, among other things, the relation between creativity, soul and soul-making, creativity is one of the five prominent groups of instinctive factors, together with reflection, activity, sexuality and hunger. Creativity is a necessity of the human life and the creative instinct is that immense energy whose origin is beyond the human psyche and which drives us to dedicate ourselves to ourselves through this and that specific medium. Creation is as much destruction as it is construction. And the notions of creativity arise empirically from a deeply felt experience, from events lived in real life, as psychic perceptions of instinctual processes (Hillman, 1979: 47-49). The Maidan, as opus of this creative force, was both destruction of the old and construction of the new, in which the 'the objectified field in the opus reacts and determines the gestalt of the creative force. The creative takes the form that is imposed on it both by the general limits of the field and by the specific limits of the opus in which it flows. The oeuvre forms the person who is in relationship with it' (Hillman, 1979: 34). Therefore, the artists created the Maidan, but the Maidan created the artists. However, 'we experience our relationship with the opus, as fulfilment and as suffering: fulfilment because in the opus the creative is contained and realized; and suffering as the limitation of each opus, of each field, tragically restricts the creative possibility within the confines of concrete realization' (Hillman, 1979: 35). And for Hillman the opus is the psyche, the soul (Hillman, 1979: 35) which is represented by a symbol: the Spirit of Maidan, the soul of Maidan.

Hence, the Maidan is a collective opus, oeuvre d'art: (1) born out from the human creative instinct in which every single artist participated in its form, shape, and meaning with his/her own artistic contribution; and (2) whose essence is represented by the symbol of the Spirit of Maidan, the soul of Maidan in which 'by soul I mean, first of all, a perspective rather than a substance, a viewpoint toward things rather than a thing itself. This perspective is reflective; it mediates events and makes differences between ourselves and everything that happens. Between us and events, between the doer and the deed, there is a reflective moment – and soul-making means differentiating this middle ground. (Hillman, 2019: 14-15)

What is more, the fieldwork reveals that the artists acted as shamans, healers, initiators, and prophets. For Campbell (1991: 122-123) shamans functioned in early societies as artists do now; they played the role of priesthood traditionally important in society. The shaman's powers are symbolized in his own familiars, deities of his own personal experience, not through a social ordination. Levi-Strauss (1963: 186-205) identifies the mechanism by which shamanistic rituals and magical symbols produce cures. However, the intervention (cure) of the shaman is to provide to the 'sick person', who believes in the myth shared within a society, with a language by means of which unexpressed, and otherwise inexpressible, psychic states can be immediately expressed. The shaman and his cure can have analogies with contemporary psychoanalysis. This relation between shaman-symbol-sick person-language creates or recreates 'the effectiveness of symbols which guarantees the harmonious parallel development of myth and action. And myth and action form a pair always associated with the duality of patient and healer [......] The effectiveness of symbols would consist precisely in this "inductive property", by which formally homologous structure, built out of different materials at different levels of life—organic processes, unconscious mind, rational thought—are related to one another' (Levi-Strauss, 1963: 201). For Morin (2016: 43-52) 'l'artiste engagé', the committed artist, of today, all the more so as he is famous and admired, is heir to a certain manner of the shaman, and also of the biblical prophet. In the creative states, shamanism brought to the extreme a way of entering the invisible, the other world—for the shaman the world of the spirits, for the artist or the author of today who has become the spirit world.

Surely, there is a spirituality in the creative process of the artists which is based on that 'inner need' pinpointed by Wassily Kandinsky: 'The inner need is built up of three mystical elements: (1) every artist, as a creator, has something in him which calls for expression. (2) Every artist, as child of his age, is impelled to express the spirit of his age—dictated by the period and particular country to which the artist belongs. (3) Every artist, as a servant of art, has to help the cause of art' (Kandinsky, 1977: 33). In this spirit, I can affirm that in Maidan 'artists were receivers and beneficiaries of signs being sent to them, more than creators. Creation comes from the artist's ability to give form to what he has received' (Berger, 2002: 18).

The artists were able (1) to translate into works of art the signs and strong emotions sent to them by a Ukrainian society and people in crisis, who were protesting against an oppressive social condition which was not offering to them any positive future to dream; and (2) to create a mythology of Maidan, because 'mythology is expression of collective unconsciousness (Campbell, 1989: 50), and the first function of a mythology is to waken and maintain in the individual a sense of wonder and participation in the mystery of this finally inscrutable universe' (Campbell, 1989: 17).

However, when analysing the 'art of Maidan', this research doesn't enter into the debate about what is art and what is not. Art, for Maruka Svasek (2007: 8-9) 'is not a straightforward descriptive category of objects with inherent qualities that can be objectively isolated and compared'. The Maidan Museum assembles objects which have been collected from the very places of the Maidan Revolution. On the whole they are classified as object art-artefacts. Although some of them can be defined as objects of art (art by intention/destination), others in their original context and purpose (art by appropriation/metamorphosis) were not intended as art objects. But they have been 'aestheticized' and then regarded as art. Svasek (2007) develops this distinction in her work, defining 'art by intention/destination', 'art by appropriation/metamorphosis' and the process of aestheticization': 'Art by intention/destination is used to refer to artefacts that were created with the specific purpose in mind that they should represent and be regarded as art by galleries and museum, and bought and sold on the art market. By contrast, art by appropriation/metamorphosis refers to objects that may have been created for a different purpose or to champion values primarily not artistic, but which subsequentlyare given the status of art and "appropriated" by museums or dealers as tradable artefacts' (Svasek, 2007: 11).

Finally, the term 'aestheticization' is used to 'conceptualise the process by which people interpret particular sensorial experiences as valuable and worthwhile. (...) The processes of aestheticization take place within and outside artistic fields of practice. (...) "aestheticization" describes the process by which objects are perceived and the ensuing sensory experience used to provide a basis for descriptions of "aesthetic experience", which in turn are used to reinforce abstract ideas and beliefs. That experience is often already influenced by additional knowledge about the object and its reported status, and by the spatial setting in which is used or displayed' (Svasek, 2007: 9-10). Therefore, the 'aesthetic experience' 'refers to a type of experience that can be similarly stimulated by religious feeling, music or even during some political rituals. A devout Catholic, for instance, could attribute an aesthetic experience stimulated by the atmosphere of a church service or religious effigy to the divine power of Christ, and use it to reinforce Christian ideals. The aestheticization of an object is thus partly derived from sensation, but is also stimulated and reinforced by other factors such as, in this case, religious belief' (Svasek, 2007: 10). Furthermore, as some informants have demonstrated during my field work, the objects which are defined as the art of Maidan underwent a 'process of beautification' meaning that their appearance was improved and they have become 'beautiful' thanks to the artists' intervention.

Therefore, all the objects presented and displayed in the Maidan Museum, whether art by intention/destination or art by appropriation/metamorphosis, went through a process of aestheticization and beautification which created the aesthetic experience of the Maidan Revolution.

The New Year Tree installation — named 'Yolka' — became a landmark revolutionary artistic space and popular open exhibit where everyone could express herself in various forms. Art and culture as alternative forms of participation in the movement enabled people to communicate their identity, values, dreams, fears, hopes, and desires for the future not only locally and nationally, but also internationally, thereby helping people worldwide to better understand their motives and their appeal to Europe. Maidan artwork projects the stories of Ukraine's identity into the wider world. Likewise, artistic creativity functioned as a form of psychotherapy, a protective and positive force for many protesters in the omnipresent violence. The Euromaidan events were able first to produce a post-colonial discourse, a new apolitical ideology based on the concepts of dignity and Ukrainian identity, second, to generate political symbols, public values and national myths; third, to create the myth of Maidan; and finally, to give birth to the Spirit of Maidan.

This post-colonial discourse is directed at and against the former colonial masters – Russia of the Tsars and of the USSR. It embodies a distinctive sense of the post-colonial which sits in an ambiguous relationship to race and racism as the anti-colonial heritage of much of eastern Europe does (distinctively in those countries which formerly lived under both Russian and Ottoman heritage). It forms a large topic which would valuably be a subject for a separate study.

The vigor and the whole of the Euromaidan events triggered a 'spirit', the so-called 'Spirit of Maidan' (in Ukrainian: дух) that completely changed the consciousness and awareness of the participants of the demonstrations. The 'Spirit of Maidan' represents the core, the soul, the breath of life of the Maidan's mythification process. Without the 'Spirit of Maidan' there would not be any Maidan myth, mythification process, rituals or any Maidan at all. Thus, the 'Spirit of Maidan' is the tangible result of the 'Maidanization process' which functioned (using a term explained above) as an emotional ritual of intensification-aggregation-initiation-passage. And the traditional cultural heritage and contemporary arts played a crucial role because they empowered the whole movement with concrete ideas, messages, identity, symbols, engagement, solidarity and understanding.

Inspired by the Revolution of Dignity, the artists created an aesthetic of Maidan, and were able to rework objects, symbols, archetypes and music already present in the Ukrainian context before the Maidan events and to give birth to renewed meanings, symbols, reinterpreted myths, canonization and interpellation. They developed a collective imaginary antagonistic to the official version, which remained anchored in the past. They created a new dimension and a new way to imagine life in Ukraine. The fictional work of Hryhorczuk, which has at its subject the Maidan events, refers to this phenomenon through the vision-diagnosis of the former Soviet communist regime (punitive medicine) as the consequences of a 'philosophical intoxication', and to 'Euromaidan madness as if it were an infectious disease' (Hryhorczuk, 2016: 20-21).

As a result, even at linguistically level, during the protests the term 'Euromaidan events' was replaced by 'the Maidan', which does not refer only to the geographic location of the Euromaidan Square (Maidan Nezalezhnosti: Independence Square), a public space in the city of Kyiv, where the demonstrations originated, but led to a new understanding of what the public practice of politics and protest mean, namely a holistic view of the signification of the events. The revolution started in Kyiv but then expanded to all Ukraine, including the territory of Donbass, and to the Crimea. This research therefore understands 'Maidan' as both the myth of Maidan and the physical place of the Museum. For this reason, it is crucial to outline the interconnected concepts of Maidan's art and of the ensuing identity discourse.

For Dr Ihor Poshyvailo, Director of the Maidan Museum, (Novinkiblog, 2016), who took the initiative to collect the artistic artefacts and stories from the field and to give birth to the Maidan Museum recognizing that Maidan art asserts itself as a form of protest. Which, in fact, did not come as a surprise given that artists and cultural activists used to be leaders in various communities expected to initiate social change. Poshyvailo talks about 'the creative force of freedom' as the specific characteristic of the '(R)evolutionary Culture of the Maidan. Equally, according to Olha Bryukhovetska of the Ukrainian Visual Culture Research Center, 'revolutionary art always comes first, not last. Revolutionary art is the one to speak about the revolution when it has not found its own words yet' (Novinkiblog, 2016).

1.2 Aims and Objectives of the Research

The purpose of this study is to understand the Maidan Museum as the 'National Memorial of the Heavenly Hundred Heroes and Revolution of Dignity Museum', and its role in preserving the Spirit of Maidan. It is therefore important to understand the meaning of the Maidan as concept and context, the importance of the art of the Maidan and its message, and the main role of the Maidan Museum.

However, first of all the Maidan (Revolution of Dignity) was a bloody identity struggle, and art played an important role in its definition, as already outlined. Identity is a human need and human identity is a cultural subject. Beyond the basic need for a sense of control, we are deeply driven by our sense of identity, of who we are. Cultural identity is essential to individuals because it gives them a sense of belonging, direction, and importance in life, and is related to nationality, ethnicity, religion, language, social class, generation, locality or any kind of social group that has its own distinct culture.

Hence, due to the vital importance identity has to human nature (and to the Maidan Revolution), I do consider the human as an 'animal identitarium', which means that his outstanding attribute and essence is a striving for identity (and the Maidan Revolution is a clear example). Humankind, different from other animals which apparently are satisfied with their one nature and identity, is in constant and anxious research and construction of his or her own identity. The 'animal identitarium' creates his or her identity through symbols, rituals, myths which become their own marks of identity; they protect it, and he/she can even kill in the name of identity (Volkan, 2006). Therefore, their identitarian symbols, rituals, and myths form an existential-revered-sacred environment and territory: his interpretative paradigm, her language and grammar, their 'real' world, are holy to them, providing meaning to life, a sense of belonging. Through these cultural creations their identity is acknowledged. And in the relative success of those creations lies a basis for securitization and insecuritization.

Therefore, inside the framework of the relation between art and identity politics, this study considers the role, the strong emotions, and the impact played by the Maidan events in the fabrication of symbols, myths, and rituals, which became essential elements in the creation of post-Euromaidan Ukrainian identity of this specific man-animal identitarium' (homo Maidan).

A critical point of the research is its search for that liminal space where the artistic activities and messages exposed by the Maidan Museum can have political repercussions. And where the latter are of such a nature that they can be represented by the political elites. This constitutes power-knowledge structures (PKS) as a security threat, because they are seen to produce (1) an alternative-antagonistic discourse of truth, power and social organization-state building; and (2) a collective imaginary divergent from the official one. Ukraine is in the middle of an identity discovering and rediscovering process in which the very notion of Ukrainian post-Soviet identity, as a national identity, is a contested concept.

For Torbakov (2018: 178) 'as soon as Ukraine gained independence following the Soviet Union's disintegration, its ultimate goal was to assert its distinct national identity and sovereignty which means, in practical terms, to attain recognition of its separateness from Russia'. In the course of this process of national identity definition and construction, strong nationalist movements and political parties wish to eradicate everything imperialistically russian and anti-Ukrainian from their country, including the old Soviet heritage, in order to produce a 'pure' Ukrainian identity, based on the imprisoned and demolished identity at the time of foreign imperial dominations and during the Great Terror. Already the 'Ukrainian nationalist historiography has come up with its own millennial narrative whereby the year 1991 — Ukraine's annus mirabilis — is presented as a glorious event on the long and thorny path of the Ukrainian people toward political independence and a national state. The major signposts of this path, this narrative asserts, are the Ukrainian ancient state of Kyiv Rus, the "Cossack State" of the 17th century and the Hetmanate of the 18th century, as well as the Ukrainian People's Republic of 1917-20. According to this linear grand story, the referendum of independence in December 1991 caps the millennium-long process of Ukrainian state — and nation-building' (Torbakov, 2018: 179).

Maidan is seen in this sense by advocates of this narrative as an apotheosis, a fulfilment of an identity immanent in historical development over the last thousand years.

Fukuyama defines the Maidan events as one of the revolutions of dignity fought around the world with the desire for the state to recognize citizens' identity and basic dignity (2018: 42-49). He is correct to see the events of the Revolution of Dignity and its commemoration as global events as well as significant in their specific local context, and one needs to remember that as one examines the detailed specifics of the Museum and its creators' interviews.

Thus, the Ukrainian identity, being a contested concept, constitutes a 'field', in the bourdieusian sense (Bourdieu, 2005), meaning a cultural, symbolic, social, spatial arena in which official agents (official power-knowledge structures) fight for power and status, and contest a new status quo. The Maidan Museum: represents a new, non-official, revolutionary and antagonist active agent inside this field; and boosts a revolutionary concept of the post-Maidan Ukrainian identity that is antagonistic to the official, still pre-Maidan Soviet-legacy Ukrainian identity, which is defined here as the official 'habitus' (Bourdieu, 2005). Understood in this way, it becomes apparent that the Maidan Museum wants to be a museum of freedom and democracy which memorializes victims and preserves artifacts of the Maidan protests but at the same time charts a course into the future, promoting basic human values and rights. Its inclusive message, which can be summarized by the concept of creativity of freedom as a 'revolutionary' impulse, is that the Ukrainian identity is not constructed on the binary-opposition linguistic division (Ukrainian-Russian), but on a common struggle for independence, dignity, and true historical memory; in summary: based on values underwritten by, or at least aspired to by, the European Union.

This text exposes ontological and epistemological dilemmas as it seeks to answer the three research questions identified already in this discussion. First, what is the Maidan Museum about? Second, when we talk about Maidan and the Spirit of Maidan, what are we talking about? And, third, what is the role of art and identity discourse in Maidan? Concurrently the research will develop the concept of the 'Maidanization process', through which the Spirit of Maidan was produced. Therefore, this research defines what 'the Maidan' is (the concept and context of Maidan). It identifies and analyzes the works of artists who participated and supported the Maidan events; inspired by the Revolution of Dignity, they produced meaningful art which became part of a new identity discourse and the mythification process of Maidan itself. And it considers the role and mission of the Maidan Museum as preserver of the 'Spirit of Maidan'. The research is organized in six chapters, of which this introductory chapter is the first.

The second chapter establishes the ontological and epistemological conundrums and identifies and defines the theories and the methodology employed in this work. The chapter introduces a multidisciplinary approach inspired by the work of

Gerard Bouchard (2017) on social myths and collective imaginaries, and the sociology of art (Alexander, 2003; Peters, 2020). Thus, 'the Maidan' is considered a metaphor and a metaphorical structure (Punter, 2007) which stands in for a 'social myth' (Bouchard, 2017). Here, social myth is understood as the combination of the five following concepts which define Maidan as a myth-metalanguage (Barthes, 2000); a spiritual place (Hryhorczuk, 2016); an anthropological place (Augé, 2011); an emotional field (Beatty, 2019); and a chosen trauma (Volkan, 1999, 2004, 2006; Svasek, 2005). The social myth is the essence of the metaphor-metaphorical structure of 'the Maidan'. Moreover, 'the Maidan' is reckoned to constitute socio-cultural-symbolic capital (Bourdieu, 2005). The research methodology draws on an established literature: Jociles Rubio, 1999; Galindo Mateo and Martin Martinez, 2007; Ercolani, 2016; Hannerz, 2010; Geertz, 1973; Navarria, 2015. It is qualitative and based on anthropological methods, including semi-structured interviews, participant observation, emic perspective, and internship at the Maidan Museum. 'Emic' here is an ethnographic term meaning to study a society or group from the inside, understanding and using its own terms and language, rather than from an external perspective. The main informants were the very artists and the personnel of the Maidan Museum. To meet the artists and the people of the Maidan Museum, to share their experiences, and to give them a voice represents the core pillar of this work. So the research can best be characterized as the result of an anthropology-ethnology of the encounter, which according to Marc Augé (2011), refers to a need, but also to pleasure linked to the sensation of movement itself. Because in this journey towards new situations and experiences 'the ethnologist is always traveling within himself: he detaches himself from his own inner self to occupy a place that is not even that of the other, but an intermediate space where he meets one or more informants, who in turn moved towards him; everyone has moved, the informer even more than the ethnologist, as he is pushed to take an unusual distance from his daily life and place himself from an observer's point of view at the limit of the unthinkable' (Augé, 2011: 95).

The third chapter 'Defining Maidan' unfolds the theoretical framework of reference using the results of the fieldwork. The chapter follows Gombrich's approach that 'there really is no such thing as art; there are only artists' (Gombrich, 1994: 4); in consequence, 'art' is conceived with reference to Moussienko's 'Art of Maidan' (2016); and to the objects, and art creations, which are now part of the Museum of Maidan. Therefore, it focuses on the artists' participation in the Maidan, on their creative processes, and on their production of 'symbols of Maidan'. The art of Maidan ('the creative force of freedom') carries an aura (Benjamin, 1973; Peters, 2020; Freeland, 2001; Dal Lago and Giordano, 2006), and is considered 'conceptual art'. The concept is that of the Maidan myth as projecting an ideology (Harris, 2008: 60-63) that is an essential element in the manufacturing of 'antagonist' collective imaginaries (Bouchard, 2017), as well as in the Maidan mythification process (Bouchard, 2017). The Maidan myth is equally essential in the social process of identity formation (Jenkins, 2014) and in showcasing the strong relationship between identity-identification-interpellation (Althusser, 1988; Ranciere, 2014).

The fourth chapter 'The Spirit of Maidan and the Maidanization Process' develops the notion of Spirit of Maidan and examines in greater detail the core concept, namely the 'Maidanization process' which has produced the Spirit of Maidan which is seen to be the result of the combination of the Maidan mythification process with the Maidan Societal Securitization ritual. Most importantly, the 'Maidanization process' is identified as the crucial antagonist socio-cultural paradigm-habitus of reference for the construction of the post-Maidan Ukrainian identity. The chapter is anchored in the interview material referred to above.

The fifth chapter is concentrated on the Maidan Museum itself, its function and its mission. The chapter makes extensive use of interviews established in Kyiv during my internship program at the Maidan Museum (June 15-23, 2019). The chapter explores the strong role of art in the production of the myth of Maidan; shows how the Museum is constructed around the Maidan myth with the specific mission to perpetuate the' Spirit of Maidan'; and defines the Maidan Museum as a social-cultural-symbolic agent.

The sixth chapter, the conclusion, affirms that the Maidan Museum is emerging as a unique and original social structure. It preserves the totality of the elements of the 'Maidanization process'. It acts as the guardian of the 'Spirit of Maidan'. It works as an agent and cultural mediator, playing a unique role in the definition of Ukrainian identity, and in cultural policy formation, all the time remaining a living monument to the relationship between art and politics, symbols and language, myths, ritual and identity formation.

2
Theoretical Framework and Methodology

This chapter defines the ontology and the epistemology of the research, and establishes the framework and the methodology employed. Crudely, the ontology is the reality of the Maidan Museum in its different physical and virtual forms, while the epistemology is the way we acquire knowledge and understanding about it.

Galindo Mateo and Martin Martinez in their text 'Atenea en el Campus – Una aproximacion a las Bellas Artes como disciplina universitaria' (2007) define three different lines of research and methodology for Fine Arts. The first line researches the concept, the second concentrates on techniques and production, and the third one investigates the artistic practices and their products. The methodology of this academic research belongs to the first line of research, and concentrates on the concept and on the context in which art is produced. Therefore, this 'research is aimed at the practices of artistic creation and their visual products, as well as the contexts in which it takes place, and has an eminently theoretical character. Its references are in disciplines of the Human and Social Sciences, such as the History of Art or Aesthetics and the Art Theory, which are usually registered in a general way in basic research' (Galindo Mateo and Martin Martinez, 2007: 56).

This research uses a multidisciplinary approach inspired by (1) the work of the sociologist Gerard Bouchard (2012) on social myths and collective imaginaries; (2) sociology of art (Alexander, 2003; Peters, 2020); and (3) the relation between anthropology, art and cultural production (Svasek, 2005, 2007, 2008, 2012). It employs first hand fieldwork experiences. It explains and establishes the theoretical framework, the interpretative paradigm, the methodology and the methods which have been used in this work. It argues that methodology 'concerns the logical structure and procedure of...enquiry' (Sartori, 2011: 11) while methods refer to

51

the different specific techniques used to collect and examine data (Crotty, 1998: 3).

This work is therefore a qualitative research project seeking to answer the main research questions of this academic work, which (to repeat) are:

1. What the Maidan Museum is about?
2. When we talk about Maidan and the Spirit of Maidan, we are talking about what?
3. What is the role of art and identity discourse in Maidan and in the Spirit of Maidan?

However, to completely grasp the full significance of the 'National Memorial of the Heavenly Hundred Heroes and Revolution of Dignity Museum', we have to look at it in the context of what Maidan is and represents, and inside the 'field' (Bourdieu, 2005) of Ukrainian identity. This is because the concept and context of the Maidan represents the social and symbolic capital, in bourdieusian sense (Bourdieu, 2005), of the Maidan Museum; the artists and their works, and the establishment of the Museum of Maidan, were inspired by Maidan; and the message which the art and the Museum want to carry and to perpetuate is about Maidan, and the essence of the post-Maidan Ukrainian identity embodied by the Spirit of Maidan.

It is not possible to analyze the Maidan Museum outside a theoretical framework which does not take in consideration the importance of elements such as power, representation, and subjectivity (Peters, 2020: 21). The Maidan events are inscribed in the category of revolutions of dignity, which have been fought around the world with the desire for the state to recognize citizens' identity and basic dignity (Fukuyama, 2018: 42-49).

Thus, it is necessary to put the elements of this work, namely the Maidan Museum, the Maidan, Art and Identity, and the Spirit of Maidan in their proper conceptual categories. This is because one must discuss meanings: the meaning of the Maidan Museum, the meaning of the Maidan, and the meaning of the art of Maidan. As will be seen below, Maidan has become a text (Geertz, 1973), the signification of which 'comes from "circulation", the interaction of texts and their perception. It is an outcome of dialogue and contended meanings. The meanings of texts are appropriated and subverted in the interests of those who consume the text. Generating meaning by subordinate classes in opposition to the dominant message is an act of defiance, semiotic resistance. The creation of meaning is a constant, and political, process. Meaning is 'a contested terrain' (Alexander, 2003: 186). On this view, the sociological discourses related to Maidan become semiotic resistance, in which 'art can have power, either through its encapsulation of ideology or in its role in discourse that work to the advantage of elites' (Alexander, 2003: 187).

What is more, revolutionary the discourse and function of the Maidan Museum must be placed inside a contending and contended arena, in which the Ukrainian identity and cultural policy are at stake. This contenting arena is represented by the concept of 'field' as developed by Bourdieu, according to whom this space is 'an autonomous universe, a kind of arena, in which people play a game which has certain rules' (Bourdieu, 2005: 215); and concurrently a 'site of struggle where individuals seek to maintain or alter the distribution of the forms of capital specific to it. The individuals who participate in these struggles will have differing aims — some will seek to preserve the status quo, others to change it — and differing chances of winning or losing, depending on where they are located in the structured space of positions' (Bourdieu, 2005: 15). And the actors-structures, which compete with each other in this field, do so using their own capital. For Bourdieu, who borrows terms from the language of economics, there are different forms of capital: not only 'economic capital' in the strict sense (i.e. material wealth in the form of money, stocks and shares, property, investment), but also 'cultural capital' (i.e. knowledge, skills and other cultural acquisitions as exemplified by educational or technical qualifications) and 'symbolic capital' (i.e. accumulated prestige or honour, social standing in a specific context). One of the most important properties of fields is the way in which they may, but do not always, allow one form of capital to be converted into another (Bourdieu, 2005: 14). Therefore, economic or material capital is not the only form of capital, and its position, power and impact depend upon its relationship to specific field of practices. According to Bourdieu cultural and symbolic forms of capital are linked to forms of power and more specifically cultural and symbolic capital is a power that is recognized. For him 'a power or capital becomes symbolic, and exerts a specific effect of domination, which I call symbolic power or symbolic violence, when it is known and recognized, that is, when it is the object of an act of knowledge and recognition' (Bourdieu, 1987: 111).

The Maidan Museum is an agent of cultural and symbolic power. For Bourdieu, that means 'a power of constituting the given through utterances, of making people see and believe, of confirming or transforming the vision of the world and, thereby, act on the world and thus ultimately it becomes a vision of the world itself. The cultural and symbolic power shows itself to be an almost magical power, which enables one to obtain the equivalent of what is normally obtained through force (whether physical or economic), by virtue of the specific effect of mobilization — is a power that can be exercised only if it is recognized, that is not identified as arbitrary. This means that symbolic power does not reside in "symbolic systems" in the form of an "illocutionary force" but that it is defined in and through a given relation between those who exercise power and those who submit to it, i.e. in the very structure of the field in which belief is produced and reproduced. What creates the power of words and slogans, a power capable in maintaining or subverting a social order, is the belief in the legitimacy of words and those who utter them. And words alone cannot create this belief' (Bourdieu, 2005: 170).

Therefore, following a bourdieusian approach, the struggle is about the essence of the Ukrainian identity seen as a 'habitus'. On one side of the field-arena, there is the official pre-Maidan Ukrainian-identity-habitus supported by its own political-knowledge apparatus (which in the following pages will be characterized as the 'zombie Sovieticus') and on the other, the antagonist side, the post-Maidan Ukrainian-identity habitus ('homo Maidan') which has its agent in the Maidan Museum. For Bourdieu 'the habitus is a set of dispositions which incline agents to act and react in certain ways. The dispositions generate practices, perceptions and attitudes which are "regular" without being consciously coordinated or governed by any "rule". The dispositions which constitute the habitus are inculcated, structured, durable, generative and transposable' (Bourdieu, 2005: 12).

In the context of the present research, the creation of imaginative pictures clearly identifies the struggle between the 'zombie Sovieticus', who wants to retain power, status quo, represents the past and belongs to the post-Soviet-Russia mind-set space, and its opposite, the 'homo Maidan' who dares to rebel against a reality and a life that is not his/her own, who embodies specific revolutionary and evolutionary expectations, who generates a vision of modernity, and belongs to the European mind-set space. As result, the power-knowledge (the 'zombie Sovieticus' and the 'homo Maidan' are regarded as two clashing PKS too) that wins the struggle (using its economic, cultural, and symbolic capitals, as capabilities) inside the field of the 'Ukrainian identity' is the one that at the end is recognized and which generates that 'Ukrainian identity knowledge', which is produced and reproduced.

The research examines the concept, context and the practices of the Maidan artistic production. This gradually evolved during the so-called Maidan events and formed a living changing force rather than a fixed 'already done' output. Maidan is thus seen as a metaphor-metaphorical structure, a concept and as a context. The theoretical framework and interpretative paradigm of reference is constructed around the definition of the metaphor-metaphorical structure 'the Maidan' as a 'social myth' (Bouchard, 2017). This theoretical approach is understood as the combination of the five following notions which define Maidan: a myth-metalanguage (Barthes, 2000); a spiritual place (Hryhorczuk, 2016); an anthropological place (Augé, 2011); an emotional field (Beatty, 2019); and a chosen trauma (Volkan, 1999, 2004, 2006; Svasek, 2005). Each of these needs to be unpacked, and their relationships understood.

At the same time, the creative process of artists who produced works of art and indeed the very creativity—the 'symbols of Maidan'—inspired by the Maidan, and the art of Maidan itself are essential elements in the manufacturing of 'antagonist' collective imaginaries (Bouchard, 2017), in the Maidan mythification process (Bouchard, 2017), in the social process of identity formation (Jenkins, 2014), in their strong showcasing of the relationship between identity, identification and interpellation (Althusser, 1988; Ranciere, 2014).

Based on the illustration of collective imaginary employed by Bouchard (2017: 13) here 'antagonist collective imaginary' is defined as all the symbols, culture, ideas, rituals and emotions produced by artists during the Maidan events. These antagonist collective imaginaries provide the base for the construction of the post-Maidan Ukrainian identity, and are antagonist to the official narrative based on a static post-soviet past. The antagonist collective imaginaries represent the answer to the question the people of Maidan were asking themselves: where do you see yourself in 10 years? And definitely, the answer of the Maidan was: not again in the Ukraine of 2013'.

This work takes into consideration the element of emotion, too, which often is excluded from the concept and idea of culture, because 'it is above all emotion—the symbols it feeds and the motivations it drives—that, when all is said and done, orients the game' (Bouchard, 2017: 11). For this reason, 'I prefer to see culture as an amalgam of (a) segments that are sometimes coherent and sometimes contradictory, but always in interaction, and (b) broad areas of indetermination' (Bouchard, 2017: 5). Ukraine is perhaps the last country of the former Soviet Union which is fighting for the construction of an independent identity and an independent culture. And in this struggle, Maidan, for its identitarian and emotional charge, can be framed inside those social, political, emotional events which constitute the geopolitics of emotion. For Dominique Moisi, who in his work has analyzed how culture of fear, humiliation, and hope are reshaping the world, 'today, quests for identity by peoples uncertain of who they are, their place in the world, and their prospects for a meaningful future has replaced ideology as the motor of history, with the consequence that emotions matter more than ever in the world where media are playing a role of a sounding board and a magnifying glass. In the larger sense, however, emotions—whether religious, national, ideological, or even purely personal—have of course always mattered' (Moisi, 2010: 4-5). We live in an age of globalization, and in order to best understand the Maidan Revolution, emotions have become indispensable to grasp the complexity of the world we live in. 'Globalization causes insecurity and raises the question of identity. (...) Identity is strongly linked with confidence, and in turn confidence, or the lack there of, is expressed in emotions—in particular, those of fear, hope, and humiliation' (Moisi, 2010: 8-12). Moisi focuses his work on three primary emotions: fear, hope, and humiliation. These very emotions were not experienced by the apathetic 'zombie Sovieticus' in the same way as were, together with dignity, the emotions which sparked the Maidan events. For Moisi these three emotions 'are closely linked with the notion of confidence, which is the defining factor in how nations and people address the challenge they face as how they relate to one another. Fear is in this sense the absence of confidence. If life is dominated by fear, one is apprehensive about the present and expects the future to become even more dangerous. Hope, by contrast, is an expression of confidence; it is based on the conviction that today is better than yesterday and that tomorrow will be better than today. Humiliation is the injured confidence of those who have lost hope in the future but feel their lack of hope is the fault of others, who have treated one badly in the past. When the contrast between your idealized and glorious past and your frustrating present is too great, humiliation prevails' (Moisi, 2010: 5). In addition, 'emotions appear to be bound up with identification' (Jenkins, 2014: 7) and if we want to understand human agency, including identification, we have to understand emotions (Jenkins, 2014: 54).

Thus, this work supports the idea that in order 'to know' and 'to understand', the researcher must 'feel' the emotions of the field-context and of the informants. My field work experience generated an overall experience which required a total immersion in the events and emotions of the 'other' (Sanmartín Arce, 2007: 59) and empathy, which aided my participant observation, let me 'feel' the 'other' (Sanmartín Arce, 2007: 63). And this brings in an important point of the anthropological work: 'probably, one of the things that differentiates the anthropologist from the practitioners of the other sciences is his special character of transmitting a personal experience' (Mira, 2007: 551). It has to be added, however, that emotions can also be regarded as valuable assets (emotional capital) that can be employed by socially situated individuals to gain power and authority (Svasek, 2008: 18).

The following chapter, 'Defining Maidan', will see the theoretical framework presented here unfolding itself, and it will match and test it with the results of the interviews, and as a result will lead to the establishment of the concept of the 'Maidanization process'. This process is understood as the combination of symbols, culture, ideas, rituals and emotions. From a purely theoretical point of view, the 'Maidanization process' is the combination of the Maidan mythification process (Bouchard, 2017) with the Maidan societal securitization ritual (Ercolani, 2016). In other words, the creation of the mythical status of Maidan coincides with the fulfilment of the ritual(s) which invest a commitment to societal security – the anticipation or at least the hope of security which holds society together. These events can be tracked in the artistic endeavours of Maidan. They necessarily happen together and in the same time and space. That complex simultaneity is captured in the unavoidably clumsy language in which it can be understood. The process created the 'Spirit of Maidan' (in Ukrainian дух), which can be characterised as the socio-cultural paradigm-habitus of reference for the construction of a post-Maidan Ukrainian identity.

The methodology of this study draws particularly on the work of Jociles Rubio, 1999, Galindo Mateo and Martin Martinez, 2007, Ercolani, 2016, Hannerz, 2010, Geertz, 1973, Augé, 2011, and Navarria, 2015. It is qualitative, based on anthropological approach which makes extensive use of semi-structured interviews, participant observation, emic perspective, and an internship at the Maidan Museum. In those interviews, the main informants were the very artists and the personnel of the Maidan Museum. In order to answer to the main research questions, in the course of a first stay in Kyiv in November 2016 and an internship period at the Maidan Museum (June 15-23, 2019), fourteen interviews were conducted and registered. The interlocutors were asked to recollect and formulate their individual participation in the Maidan events, in the ensuing creative processes, and in the production of the 'symbols of Maidan'. In short, they were asked to reproduce verbally and reflect on 'their Maidan'.

This research framework was that of social anthropology applied to a Fine Arts topic, and this because social anthropology 'is primarily about social relationships; only derivatively, and not necessarily, about places' (Hannerz, 2010: 67). Therefore, the most important elements in this research come from my informants. They were: Ihor Poshyvailo (Director Maidan Museum), Oles Kromplias (artist, photographer and war correspondent), Ekateryna Romanova (Head of the Research Department, Maidan Museum), Tatyana Cheprasova (artist, painter), Taras Kompanichenko (artist, musician), Oleksander Ivanovych Melnyk (artist, painter), Ivan Semesyuk (artist, poet, musician author), Sasha Komyakhov (artist, freelance illustrator), Yuriy Gruzinov (documentary cinema operator, winner of the Shevchenko Prize in 2018), Neda Nedjana (playwright and director), Yulia Ovcharenko (artist, illustrator), Valery Hladunets (folklorist, singer, cultural manager), Glib Viches (artist, curator, lecturer in Cultural Studies), Maryna Sochenko (artist and teacher at the Ukrainian Art Academy).

The social relations between these activists and with the author, including time spent with the informants as well as correspondence by email after initial interviews, aimed at exploring their feelings and the emotions clearly present in their memories. These provided the material which has been essential to defining the myth of Maidan, its message, the function of art, to identify the symbols of Maidan, the essence of the Spirit of Maidan, and the role of the Maidan Museum.

Therefore, to analyze the Maidan as a metaphor-metaphorical structure, a concept and a context necessitated a 'sorting out the structure of signification—what Ryle called established codes, a somewhat misleading expression, for it makes the enterprise sound too much like that of a cipher clerk when it is much more like that of a literary critic—and determining their social ground and import' (Geertz, 1973: 9). For Geertz' ethnography is thick description. What an ethnographer is in fact faced with is a multiplicity of complex conceptual structures, many of them superimposed upon, or knotted into one another, which are at once strange, irregular, and inexplicit, and which must contrive somehow first to grasp and then to render (...) Doing ethnography is like trying to read (in the sense of "construct a reading of") a manuscript—foreign, faded, full of ellipses, incoherencies, suspicious emendations, and tendentious commentaries, but written not in conventionalized graphs of sound but in transient examples of shaped behavior' (Geertz, 1973: 9-10).

As a result of this approach, the researcher-ethnographer enters into the metaphor-metaphorical structure of 'Maidan': 'Maidan' becomes a 'manuscript' which the researcher-ethnographer needs to read, to decode, to understand, to feel, and to translate. Then, it is important to define the position of the reader, and the weight of the concept of 'thick description' in this context.

A specific reading strategy of 'Maidan' has been adopted here in order to produce knowledge. Umberto Eco distinguishes the empirical reader and the model reader: for Eco the empirical reader means any given, concrete reader reading a text, one of the many concrete actualizations of the abstract notion of the reader. The model reader, instead, is one who, apart from the author, is able to interpret a text in a similar way to the author who generated it. 'The author has thus to foresee a model of the possible reader (the model reader) supposedly able to deal interpretatively with the expressions in the same way as the author deals generatively with them' (Eco, 1995: 7). For the reader to become a 'model reader', it is necessary to fulfil 'a whole [set] of happiness conditions, textually established, which has to be satisfied in order to have the text fully actualized in its potential content' (Eco, 2006: 62). To become an effective reader of the Maidan narratives of the artists and activists he met, the researcher approached the Maidan metaphor-metaphorical structure, concept-context through the narrative reading, through the experiences of interactions with informants and as an empirical reader who had the good fortune to move around the places where the events of Maidan took place.

As already noted, drawing from Geertz, one of the main analytical tools of an interpretative understanding is 'thick description'. In ethnography the problem is represented by a translation, which is not only a linguistic translation, but a more complete effort that include body language, metaphors, emotions, and an effort to identify and deconstruct complex relations. Geertz provides a description of what he considers 'thick description' when he analyses Ryle's example of 'two boys rapidly contracting the eyelids of their right eye. In one, this is an involuntary twitch; in the other, a conspiratorial signal to a friend. The two movements, are, as movements, identical; (...) yet the difference (...) between a twitch and a wink is vast; (...) The winker is communicating, and indeed communicating in a quite precise and special way, deliberately, to someone in particular, to impart a particular message, and according to a socially established code. As Ryle points out, the winker has not done two things, voluntarily contracting his eyelids and winking—he has communicated through a public code which can be understood as conspiratorial. The twitcher has done only one thing, involuntarily contracting his eyelids. From this basic account Ryle moves to a fuller range of signals and meanings, a stratified hierarchy in terms of which twitches, winks, fake-winks, parodies, rehearsals of parodies are all potentially perceived and interpreted' (Geertz, 1973: 6-7).

However, to look at this anthropological experience only as a text, a manuscript, exclude one of the main points of this work which defines Maidan as an emotional field. In the Maidan, emotions have oriented the game, and 'the principal way in which we are interpellated is through metaphor, and also that we are interpellated as metaphor' (Punter, 2007:42). Therefore, as suggested by Andrew Betty (2019) what is needed is a 'deep description', which is 'a firmer sense of presence, a counter to the smiley' (Beatty, 2019: 15), and that considers the interpellation-emotional side of the metaphorical field-text.

Indeed, what an ethnographer does is to look, to see and to feel, where it is possible, an event-reality in a different way. For John Berger 'seeing comes before words. It is seeing, which establishes our place in the surrounding world; we explain that world with words, but words can never undo the fact that we are surrounded by it. The relation between what we see and what we know is never settled' (Berger, 1972: 7). In the analysis of the Maidan concept, the ethnographer, using the tool of thick description and deep description, posits himself/herself between what she/he sees and what she/he knows, between the observation of the Maidan event, the theory (the official narrative which defines Maidan), and the emotion that accompany and envelop the maidan. She/he 'reads' a reality, an event, a social fact as if it was a text, and in feeling it (through the first-hand experience of his/her informants) and interpreting it, sorts out those structures of signification and determines their social ground and import. It is there, that the results of his/her field work provide the qualitative elements which contribute to define the Maidan knowledge. At least, 'a good interpretation of anything—a poem, a person, a history, a ritual, an institution, a society—takes us into the heart of that of which is the interpretation' (Geertz, 1973: 18). It is during the participant observation that it is possible to practice the anthropological gaze (Ercolani, 2016; Jociles Rubio, 1999) which unveils the 'emic' perception because it is an engaged gaze with the human experience of the informants. That is, a dialogue not only of words, but of eyes and feelings.

However, it must be said that the fieldwork of this research has been a difficult one because of the strong and dramatic emotions attached to the events of Maidan in which my informants participated, experiencing violence and the death of friends. Most of the time, during the interviews, the informant was taken by his/her emotions, and tears were appearing on his/her face, the hands were trembling, and some time the informant's gaze was lost far away in his/her emotional memories. These interviews were stressful and painful for the informants, who wanted at the same time, to pass his/her first-hand experiences to me and to my interpreter, Ms. Dara Sereda.

The next chapter 'Defining Maidan' will unveil the theory, the concepts, and the methodology employed in this work in the context of Maidan and the results of my field work. Employing a comparative approach, every concept and theory has been tested and confronted with the firs-hand experiences of my informants.

3
Defining Maidan

3.1 Introduction

'When we talk about Maidan, we are talking about what?'. If there is not an undisputable answer to this question, the framework of the research collapses as it loses its concreteness.

The Maidan Nezalezhnosti (Independence Square; figure 2) in Kyiv is a public space, however, when Ukrainians talk about and refer to 'the Maidan' they allude not only to a physical place in Kyiv, the capital of Ukraine, but also to 'the Maidan' events in their dramatic totality. Maidan is a public space but is a 'contested space' (Wilson, 2020: 75) as the Revolution on Granite (1990), the Orange Revolution (2004) and the Revolution of Dignity (2013-2014) have demonstrated. As Jaffe and De Koning (2016) have argued, 'there is a relation between political mobilization and public space. 'Monumental spaces, such as central squares, boulevards, national assemblies or courthouse, suggest particular relations between the state and citizens. While these sites are intended to convey and produce particular relations of power, their symbolic associations with the state and ruling elites also make them important arenas for the   contestation of dominant political representations. (…) Large demonstrations with witty or rousing slogans, with a carnivalesque or sober and serious atmosphere, can become counter-spectacles that question, ridicule and undermine the legitimacy of powerful actors. Visibility is a key aspect of the political potential of public space. It allows groups of people to present their political views, often by the force of sheer numbers, position themselves as representatives of large collective. Pitching their views and concerns as those of a large collectivity, most often the nation, allows protesters to question the legitimacy of state politics, which are often times also formulates with reference to the will or the welfare of "the people". Public spaces incapital or major cities are especially effective arenas for thistype of self-representation, since these spaces are most readly associates with the nation' (Jaffeand De Koning, 2016: 146-147).

Figure 2. Maidan Square. (Photo credit: G. Ercolani, 2019)

Maidan, in this process of political mobilization and of revolutions, has become from a contested public space a metaphor-metaphorical structure constructed as social myth (a myth-metalanguage, a spiritual place, an anthropological place, an emotional field, and a chosen trauma); in this creative process the artists played a fundamental role and they shaped the Maidan as an 'aesthetic experience' (Svasek, 2007: 10).

At the end, the Revolution of Dignity has demonstrated that 'Maidan' and 'the Maidan' have become synonymous with the Ukrainian way to defend personal and civil freedoms against injustice, human rights and dignity deterioration, governmental corruption, tyranny and despotism. Figure 3 shows the chaotic history of Kyiv's protest through one of the maps produced by Dmytro Vortman.

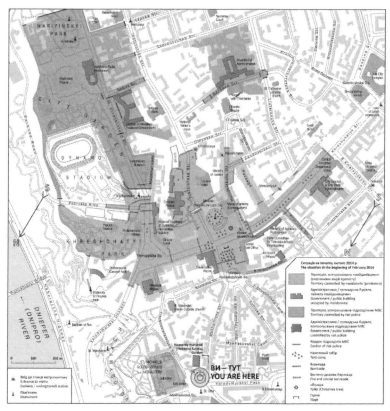

Figure 3. Map of the Maidan events in Kyiv, courtesy of the Maidan Museum

3.2. Defining Maidan as a Social Myth: Myth-Metalanguage, Spiritual Place, Anthropological Place, Emotional Field, and Chosen Trauma

'Maidan' is a metaphor-metaphorical structure which stands in for a 'social myth' which is understood as the combination of the five following concepts: Maidan as myth-metalanguage; as a spiritual place; as an anthropological place; as an emotional field; and as a chosen trauma.

Maidan as a social myth: when I met Ivan Semesyuk (artist, poet, musician author; founder of Artistic Barbican; figure 4), one of the very 'creators' of Maidan, I asked him the same question 'when we talk about Maidan, what we are talking about? Ivan's answer was straight forward: 'I influenced Maidan, I have a blog with more than 30.000 followers, and I am always protesting with my art. I consider Maidan a big art project. We were the creators of Maidan. For some people Maidan was enlightening. To me Maidan was as emotional shock, this is because it started the very day that various coincidences happenedto me: my own birthday (November 21); the closing of my Zhlob-Art exhibition; and the beginning of Maidan Revolution. In this sense Maidan was for me a mystical moment. I was one of the founders of the Barbican movement and place, which now continuous to exist but more like a bar and a concert place. I consider Maidan the moment of truth, the biggest art project in which I participate in my life'. And for Ivan 'Maidan is a magic place. Maidan is a fairytale with a good end'.

Figure 4. Ivan Semesyuk. (Photo credit: G. Ercolani, 2019)

In this creative and aesthetic experience which involved various artists Oleksandr Ivanovych Melnyk recalls how, together with his artist friends, after the opening of the 'Second Freedom' exhibition, in the hall of the Mohyla Art Academy in Podil (Kyiv), they decided to join the Maidan: 'we went to Maidan to support the students. There in Maidan assemblies were organized where people were taking decisions. I went there with my colleagues. We were millions and millions in the square, and I said "let's doing something to show to the people that we artists support their actions." And we brought our work of arts to Maidan. When the first time I went to Maidan with my works, because there were not easels, I was holding my picture with my hands. There were artists from all Ukraine and everybody was holding their work of arts like me. There were journalists who were curious and they started asking questions, and to make a video'.

Being myself a sociocultural anthropologist, Ivan and Oleksandr answers, paired with my research and experiences during visits and fieldwork in Kyiv, as well as the internship at the Maidan Museum, brought to my mind the idea that Maidan is a myth: Maidan has become a myth, and more precisely a 'social myth', which is a story that conveys symbolic truths about how a particular group experiences the world.

Bouchard defines social myth as 'a collective representation that is hybrid, beneficial, or harmful, imbued with the sacred, governed by emotion more than by reason, and a vehicle of meanings, values, and ideals shaped in a given social and historical environment. Among these attributes, sacredness is the most decisive (...). It is sacredness that mainly distinguishes myth from other collective representations' (Bouchard, 2017: 25). In Maidan that sacredness is engendered both by the sacrifice of the individuals who are commemorated and through the struggle to create art/artefacts which connect the events of the recent past to the viewer's lived experience. It has religious connotations especially for those to whom religious belief is important, but it is no less 'sacred' to an entirely secular viewer.

Therefore, under the umbrella term of 'social myth', I incorporate the five concepts identified before: Maidan as a myth-metalanguage, as a spiritual place, as an anthropological place, as an emotional field, and a chosen trauma. This follows because, following Bouchard, I situate the phenomenon of the myth inside the universe of collective imaginaries and because social myths are representations that are key elements of collective imaginaries (Bouchard, 2017: 4). For Bouchard 'we consider myth as a type of collective representation (sometimes beneficial, sometime harmful), as a vehicle of what I would call a message—that is, of values, beliefs, aspirations, goals, ideals, predispositions, or attitudes' (Bouchard, 2017: 23). It is the specificity of the sacredness of the myth, of the collective representation (vehicle of a message), and the driving power of emotions that add another element to the consideration of Maidan as a social myth. This argument builds equally on the concepts of 'myth-sacredness', 'collective representation-vehicle-message', and 'emotions' in the notion of myth of Barthes (2000), in the idea of spiritual place of Hryhorczuk (2016), in the theory of anthropological place of Augé (2011), in the emotions in the field (Beatty, 2019), and in the role of chosen trauma (Volkan, 1999, 2004, 2006; Svasek, 2005).

Maidan as a myth-metalanguage: Roland Barthes (2000: 109) holds that the myth is a system of communication defined as a 'second order semiological system' in which a power-knowledge structure plays a fundamental role. For Barthes, the 'first order semiological system' is formed by the 'Signifier' (acoustic image), the 'Signified' (concept) and the 'Sign' (relation between concept and image) (Barthes, 2000: 109-117). This first order represents a linguistic system, which, once applied to the term 'Maidan', unpacks these following results. The Signifier is the written word 'Maidan', while the 'Signified' is represented by the etymological meaning of 'Maidan', which in Ukrainian means 'square', and it is normally used to define the main square of a city, in the case of Kyiv its central square, Maidan Nezalezhnosti (Independence Square), so the 'Signified' is 'Maidan-square'. Finally, 'Sign' is what is here called 'Maidan', meaning the myth of Maidan; this constitutes the 'referent' in this work, namely the Maidan-myth.

The myth, however, is a peculiar system because it is constructed from a semiological chain which existed before it: it is, in Barthes' sense, a second order semiological system. What is a sign (the associative total of a concept and an image) in the first system becomes a mere signifier in the second. The material of mythical speech, however different at the start, is reduced to a pure signifying function as soon as they are caught by myth. And when encompasses only alphabetical or pictorial writing, myth conceives of these only as a sum of signs, a global sign, the final term of a first semiological chain. And it is precisely this final term which will become the first term of a greater system.

This lateral shift is essential for the analysis of myth. In the myth there are two semiological systems, one of which is staggered in relation to the other: a linguistic system, the language, which Barthes calls language-object, because it is the language which myth utilizes to build its own system; and myth itself, which Barthes calls a 'metalanguage', because it is a second language in which one speaks about the first. When she reflects on a metalanguage, the semiologist no longer needs to ask herself questions about the composition of the language-object, she no longer has to take into account the details of the linguistic schema. She will only need to know its total term, or global sign, and only as this term lends itself to myth. This is why the semiologist is entitled to treat writing and pictures in the same way: what he or she retains from them is the fact that they are both signs and that they constitute a language-object.

Thus, the 'metalanguage' is a product of the cultural context. Every cultural context creates and fabricates its own 'metalanguage' which is based on the symbolic interpretation of reality and is expressed through the use of myths. The symbols that integrate into the myths do not have a literary-linguistic meaning but their significance have their roots in the cultural context, and they are conveyed through the employment of the 'metalanguage'.

Therefore, the 'second order semiological system' of the myth of Maidan is made up of: 'I SIGNIFIER' is provided by '3. Sign' (Maidan-myth)'; 'II SIGNIFIED' is the result of the political, intellectual, elaboration of 'Maidan-square' by an epistemological community-power-knowledge structure; and 'III SIGN' is the characteristic and peculiar image/picture that the sign will assume which changes in time and space.

As a result, while in the linguistic system the word 'Maidan' has only one referent represented by its etymological meaning 'Maidan-square', in the metalanguage system (the myth of Maidan) the term 'Maidan' is the result of a linguistic-narrative fabrication and of power struggle, which can change with time and space. A 'Maidan knowledge' is constructed around this 'myth' of Maidan, which, depending on the political forces in power, creates its 'truth' and 'reality' which employs the authorized and the authoritative language (Bourdieu, 2005: 107-116). The work in Maidan and, more broadly, the Spirit of Maidan carry a unique authority because of this transformation.

In this specific context, the step from the first to the second semiological order, which represents the very fabrication of the myth Maidan, has been possible only by the protests, the dramatic events, and the impact they had on its linguistic use. For Womack 'myths describe the nature of the universe, both natural and supernatural, and define the place of human beings within this symbolic landscape. In many cases, the symbolic landscape conforms in a general way to the physical landscape occupied by the group that has given rise to the myth. The myth describes the landscape in term of its meaning for the people who occupy it. A myth also defines the obligations people owe to each other; to the plants, animals, and geographical features that make up the landscape; and to the spirit entity or beings that created the landscape and established the order of the universe' (Womack, 2005: 80-81).

Already in the past, even before 2013, Maidan square was occupied during the student hunger strike called the 'Revolution on Granite' (1990), the 'Ukraine without Kuchma' mass protest (1999-2000), and the Orange Revolution (2004). But with the Maidan events and the killing of more than one hundred demonstrators, the term Maidan (Maidan myth) has become fully synonymous of the Revolution of Dignity (November 21, 2013 – February 23, 2014). Maidan can be defined in the same way as the 'Place de la Bastille' (Paris, France –in the Revolution of 1789) or, according to Sophie Pinkham, who witnessed the demonstrations, 'a kind of Black Square, a ground zero. Maidan is the place where history ends and returns and begins, the moment of liberation that lays bare the uncertainty of the future. (…) The Black Square evokes both utopian dreams and the threat of anarchy. Malevich's icon was worshipped by some, but denounced by others as a "sermon of nothingness and destruction"' (Pinkham, 2016: xiii, evoking the revolutionary impact of the art of the Russian revolution). Or even the 'holy corner' of new Ukraine (through the performance of Glib Viches). Thus, the 'Black Square-ground zero-holy corner' where the consciousness of new Ukraine and the new Ukrainian identity has born out of a bloody struggle. A new identity that is strongly soliciting dignity, which means, according to the Concise Oxford English Dictionary, 'the state or quality of being worthy of honour or respect' (Stevenson and Waite, 2012: 401).

For this reason, the power of the myth of Maidan cannot be seen only inside a system of communication (myth-metalanguage). But Maidan becomes a creation myth too, because something concrete has been created there: the new Ukrainian identity. According to Womack 'creation myths are symbolically stories describing how the universe and its inhabitants came to be. Creation myths develop through oral traditions and therefore typically have multiple versions. Variations in a particular creation myth reflect differences of language and regional affiliations. Though they may appear to be simply adventure stories about things that happened in the past, creation myths continue to have relevance by providing a social charter in describing how human society came to be' (Womack, 2005: 81). Thus, the above reinforces the argument sustained in this research that Maidan represents the inspirational events of the creative process of the artists of Maidan. Whether one says that Maidan gives birth to a wholly new identity or offers a re-forging of existing contended identities, there is no doubt something new has appeared.

Maidan as a spiritual place: Hryhorczuk, in his fictional book 'Myth and Madness', blends magical realism with historical events on the Maidan in order to tell a modern-day fairy tale of Ukraine's quest for identity. Father Ilarion, a fictional character in the novel, says: 'the Maidan is a spiritual place. Whether you believe in God the Father or not, you can't deny that the spirit is at work here. It's a struggle of good versus evil, as old as time itself' (Hryhorczuk, 2016: 44). The same representation is reflected in the pages of Anna Reid's book 'Borderland — A Journey Through the History of

Ukraine' (2015), which is dedicated to the Maidan, where 'Priests —
Orthodox and Uniate together — appeared on stage every evening,
leading the crown in prayers. (Yanukovic was told to repent of his
crimes, the crowd to repent of paying and receiving bribes)' (Reid,
2015: 262). And those prayers can be considered a collective
representation, too, staged in Maidan. This is the point made by
Kozak, who sees the Maidan as a stage, a grand public work of
process art with a cast of several thousand (Kozak, 2017: 9).

Kozak describes the staging process and the surreal alteration
of the Maidan space by the construction of barricades: 'an
enormous assemblage constructed from salvaged urban materials,
which, in order to secure protestors from police violence, enclosed
the square in early December 2013. (…) The barricades transformed
the square into a fortress. The new identity of the place was
underlined with the protest "tower", a metal cone more than one
hundred foot high composed of vertical bound by horizontal circles
and subsumed in a miscellaneous carpet of flags. (…) Its framework
came from an unfinished city Christmas tree which the authorities
installed on the square each year for the holiday season' (Kozak,
2017: 16).

Maidan is then a spiritual place, a sacred space in which the
artists acted as shamans, healers, initiators, and prophets, and a
human transformation took place; in which the soul of the
participants acquired a different dimension and level of
consciousness, because it 'is sacredness that mainly distinguishes
myth from other collective representations' (Bouchard, 2017: 25).
This transformed Maidan, as a spiritual place into an aesthetic
experience (Svasek, 2007: 10).

However, the Maidan was the site of a bloody confrontation
in which more than one hundred demonstrators lost their lives
(figure 5).

Figure 5. Memory site of the Heroes of the Heavenly Hundred.
(Photo credit: G. Ercolani, 2016)

Between January 16, 2014, when Yanukovich imposed a 'dictatorship law', which because of the confrontation with the police caused the protests to turn into nightly near-riots, and February 20, 2014, which was the bloodiest day of the clashes, it is now reckoned 107 civilians were killed. The participants in the Revolution of Dignity, who were killed by the security officers and their mercenaries, were given the name of the 'Heavenly Hundred'. The name Heavenly Hundred contains an allusion to the Cossack XVIIth century army 'Sotnia' ('Hundred') companies, who were recreated as divisions of task forces at the Maidan protests. They were people of different nationalities, age groups, genders, education background, from various regions of Ukraine and from abroad, successful entrepreneurs and poor pensioners, scientists, artists, students, and activists. The youngest, Nazarii Voitovych, was seventeen. The oldest, Ivan Nakonechnyi, was eighty-two (Reid, 2015: 264-268; Plokny, 2015: 339).

The Ukrainian writer Andrei Kurkov, in his 'Diari Ucraini' (2014) leaves a dramatic description of the terrible and bloody events of those days.

The same strong emotions were present during my interviews because my informants were present in Maidan in that period.

Therefore, the same concept of Maidan as a fortress and as the site of struggle between good and evil, is aesthetically experienced and communicated through a religious symbolism (and the use of the color 'black' to define the evil forces) in the visual works and language of artists involved with the Maidan Museum.

Examples include the work of Vasyl Korchynskyi (figure 6), preserved in the temporary offices of the Maidan Museum, which transmits the sensation that the Maidan protestors were fighting against the forces of Evil.

On one side of the painting there are the protestors supported in their struggle by angels, whereas on the opposite side we can see the black figures (riot police) which symbolize the force of evil.

Figure 6. Detail of 'Maidan' by Vasyl Korchynskyi, courtesy of the Maidan Museum

The performance of one of the informants-interviewees, Oleksandr Ivanovych Melnyk, carries the same meaning.

Oleksandr joined Maidan (figure 7) when the police started attacking and beating the students (November 21, 2013) and he joined the protest carrying one of his works, namely a canvas with human eyes which recalls the gaze of Jesus or God in various religious icons.

Figure 7. 'I can see your deeds', courtesy of Oleksandr Ivanovych Melnyk

His work is called 'I can see your deeds' (figure 8) which is written (in Ukrainian) in front of the canvas, whilst on the back is written, always in Ukrainian, 'You are beautiful, I love you' (figure 9).

Figure 8. 'I can see your deeds'. (Photo credit: G. Ercolani, 2019)

Figure 9. 'You are beautiful, I love you' (Photo credit: G. Ercolani, 2019)

'I can see your deeds' was not created specifically for Maidan, but it was exposed in the hall of the Art Academy in Kyiv. This is how Oleksandr recalls his performance in Maidan: 'when this work was in the hall of the Art Academy my work meant that God can see the behaviour of all human beings. When I brought the work to Maidan, it was pointed to the direction of the Berkut-Police: God's eyes were looking at the police forces and at Yakunovich. In a way, the meaning of my work it did not change because God is looking at the behaviour of human beings in general, but the gaze of God became pointed. And the main messages were to remind the Berkut-police that God was looking at what they were doing, and that they would pay a prize for their wrong doing. In Maidan there were stages where politicians came to speak, therefore, I was reminding them that they took a oath in defending the people, and God was there looking at this. And the message (figure 9) on the back of the canvas-sign ('You are beautiful, I love you') was meaning that God was loving the people, He was loving them. About my canvas-sign, the image reproduced in it is not of any God in particular, or Jesus, he represents some higher power, someone-something who was watching'. Importantly, the picture bears two holes made by bullets fired by snipers.

Maryna Sochenko, teacher at the Ukrainian Art Academy, invited me in her studio, in the outskirt of Kyiv, in a typical Soviet style building. Her studio was congested with her paintings. She did more than two hundred paintings during Maidan, where she spent all her time among the protesters, and her main purpose was to document the events: 'a lot of my paintings are in the Maidan Museum. I came to Maidan because something good was happening in a country full of corruption. I did around 200 paintings during the Maidan events. However, coming to Maidan I understood that the political elites consider the human beings like nothing, for them they are just bodies, flesh. My personal struggle with the corruption started before Maidan because I am a member of human rights association'. Maryna did portraits of protesters, and of dead protesters. And this specific canvas (figure 10) renders clearly the struggle between the forces of Evil (wearing black uniforms) against the forces of dignity: 'look at this work. In this picture the man bitten by the police, a Polish journalist, recognized himself in my exhibition. I did this work when the BERKUT charged the students. And the signs you see on the canvas are real, they were there in Maidan, and my son was in Maidan too'.

Figure 10. 'Maidan' by Maryna Sochenko. (Photo credit: G. Ercolani, 2019)

The same theme (figure 11) of the struggle of good versus evil is expressed visually in this painted shield, used during the Maidan by some protestors to protect themselves against attacks by the Berkut (riot police). The shield, stored in the Maidan Museum office, shows a white dove fighting a black crow, and a verse of the national poet Taras Schevhenkois reproduced on it: 'Борітеся-поборете, вамБогпомагає' (Fight, fight, God helps you).

Figure 11. Detail of painted shield 'Борітеся-поборете, вамБогпомагає'
(Fight, fight, God helps you), courtesy of the Maidan Museum

Yulia Ovcharenko, a young artist, participated to the Maidan as
member of the artistic organization 'Mystetska Sotnia' ('Artistic
Hundreds'): 'I have my personal story on how I joined this artistic
organization. I came to Maidan with a group of friends. At that

moment not many people supported the protestors in Maidan. Personally, I did not know anything about Maidan, and I did not speak to the protestors. And I read on Facebook that a group of artists were gathering in the Ukranian House. Therefore, I decided to join this group with the aim to contact them, to share ideas with these creative people. Basically, I wanted to meet artists, and to meet someone able to understand me. The artists there were apolitical; they were not affiliated to any political organization or creed. So, I joined this group and I entered in contact with others artists. It was a very interesting experience because I met people coming from different regions of Ukraine, and it was a fantastic opportunity to me to know something new. And finally, in Maidan, I met the man who is now my husband (who comes from a region outside Kyiv). My husband is not an artist, and during the Maidan event he was a professional military. Thus, while I was staying in the Ukrainian House, I started to work on some religion images (icon style). This was something new to me. People were coming to me and asked to produce religious images for them'.

While there, Yulia started to paint shields, too, with the intention to produce amulets with the power to protect the protestors. This shield (figure 12), which she painted, represents Saint Michael the Archangel (Архангел Михаїл; Arkhanhel Mykhail), one of the supreme angels in Christian belief. Ukrainians share many of the Christian beliefs about Saint Michael, particularly about his leading role in the struggle against Satan — hence, the name Arkhystratyh Mykhail 'the Supreme Commander Michael.' He was believed to have taken thunder away from Satan and handed it over to Saint Elijah. Ukrainians adopted Saint Michael as the patron saint of hunters and the city of Kyiv.

Figure 12. Painted shield 'Saint Michael the Archangel' by Yulia Ovcharenko, courtesy of the Maidan Museum

Yulia's work participated in the aestheticitisation and beautification process of objects now part of the art of Maidan: 'the mission of the "Artistic Hundred" was to produce artistic objects. The protestors came to us and asked to print their shields. The protestors talked to the artists and after that the artists produced an image, most of the time based on the experience narrated by the protestors. I recall my own experience. I remember a protestor, his name was Maxim. He was coming from a region out of Kyiv. He had problem with his family that doid not support his views. And he had a sister in Kyiv, she was a student, and she was beaten during the demonstration. I listened to his story, to his experience, and then I elaborated an image for his shield. The message on the shield says: "Unite our hearts and be strong", in unity strength' (figure 13).

Figure 13. Painted shield "Unite our hearts and be strong"by Yulia Ovcharenko, courtesy of the Maidan Museum

Another artist who contributed with her work to enrich the symbolism of Maidan as a spiritual place and aesthetic experience was Tatyana Cheprasova.

In emotional interviews, she was able to externalize and transmit the dramatic emotions she experienced during her participation in Maidan: 'in Maidan I saw two opposite things: death and life. And both energies, the energy of death and the energy of life, were there. There was a struggle between life and death in Maidan. Maidan was like a ritual where energy was produced. And energy was produced by the struggle between life and death. The energy of Maidan is the energy of life. Maidan was a special event. People were not afraid to die. People took part at the Maidan events and they were not afraid to die, and I saw it, and I saw how people became open to everything. The authorities started to act against the people in Maidan because they were shocked by this energy. People came to Maidan and they drunk the wine of energy, and they were transformed. My former studio was very close to the Maidan events and I was always walking there. And I felt the energy there, and I felt the fear of these people who did not know what was going on Maidan was like an explosion in Ukraine. In Ukraine there is a before and after Maidan time. Maidan is energy, Maidan is life. Energy and Dignity. Dignity is Energy. I saw the Feb. 17th and 18th (2014) events in Maidan, I saw the shit in Maidan. Everybody has God and Evil inside himself'.

Her painted helmets with their specific religious symbolism are a clear example of how the Maidan was perceived and lived. Tatyana reproduces a picture of Caravaggio on a helmet (figure 14) in which we can see Judas kissing Jesus.

Figure 14. Tatyana Cheprasova showing her 'Caravaggio' painted helmet.
(Photo credit: G. Ercolani, 2019).

The reference to a religious symbol is clear; Tatyana, however, told me that she tried to bring 'beauty' to the Maidan. Maidan was brute violence, while 'beauty' was a sorely missing human element. And she 'aestheticized' and 'beautified' rough material brought from Maidan with religious images as the case of her triptych (figure 15): 'I remember this was during the Easter period. I went to Maidan and I saw these wooden boards on which the demonstrators were sleeping. Maidan, for me was like a big family. This was after the big tragic events of Feb 2014. The tents were still present in the square, and the Maidan event lasted until August 2014. However, after Easter 2014, the general environment changed drastically, and the people that gathered in Maidan were different from the original people. There were poor people, violence, etc., political extreme groups, etc... Basically all the intellectuals have disappeared. This was a time of intense political activity and was the time of the Crimean crisis. I remember a Cossack became very aggressive against me because the Christ on my board was too Jew for him.....they, the Cossacks are against Jews'.

Figure 15. Tatyana Cheprasova'striptych, courtesy of the Maidan Museum

Music too contributed to the aesthetic experience of Maidan as a spiritual place. Valery Hladunets (folklorist, singer, cultural manager; figure 42) recalls how he joined Maidan together with his music group: 'I joined and supported Maidan from the beginning. I came to Maidan square with my music group and we started playing and singing in Maidan underground. Then we proposed to organize traditional Ukrainian folk dance classes. This traditional Ukrainian folk music and dance are based on cappella music, chorus-voices and instrumental music. Therefore, our proposal was supported and very well welcomed and a lot of people came to start dancing Ukrainian folk music. The Maidan underground was a big space for enough people. At the same time there were tents in front of the Ukrainian house and we gave concerts there. After the students' beating all the artists we came together and we gather and we made "one" big tents city in Maidan square. In this tent city in Maidan square, we were using as a symbol only the blue and yellow colour of the Ukrainian flag and the very Ukrainian flag. All the protestors had to be apolitical and only united for the Ukrainian independence. However, in Maidan square there was more politics than everywhere in Kyiv. With my group we proposed to organize a night duty. People agreed and we organized all night concerts and performances on the main stage in Maidan square. People were singing, playing music, dancing Ukrainian folk songs, etc. One very famous artist, i.e., performed at 5 a.m. Basically, this was the way to "survive the night". At the same time, we did not have clear information about the situation around the city. There were a lot of gossips, and rumours.

The playwright and director Neda Nedjana, in her play 'Maidan Inferno or The Other Side of Hell' (figure 16), employs the image of fire and flames to evoke the spirituality of Maidan and the image of the Manichean struggle between the forces of good and evil. She participated in Maidan, and her play, written in the spring of 2014, is part of several realities. The first is that of Euromaidan, with its students, a musician, a journalist, a nurse, a priest, who take part in the actions of protests against the crimes of the government then in place. The second is that of the characters' inner monologues, their feelings, and their reflection on the situation. Finally, the third reality is virtual: it is that of social networks. Behind the fights and the crossed destinies, was a movement of evolution, which deeply modified the mentalities of all. In the play Neda refers to the Myth of Orpheus and Eurydice; but in her case, it is Eurydice who is searching for Orpheus in the 'Inferno'. Maidan becomes the fortress of freedom, while outside Maidan there is 'Inferno' (hell), and the protesters are protected by the flames of fire. Neda remembers the night of February 18-19, 2014, the bloody one, as a night of catharsis; people around her started singing the national anthem and they were all crying. The image Neda creates in her play is that of the fortress of Maidan, which, encircled by fire that protects the protesters, becomes a spiritual place.

Figure 16. Cover of the 'Maidan Inferno' play, courtesy of Neda Nedjana.

The Manichean struggle is likewise strongly present in the documentary of Yuriy Gruzinov's 'Babylon 13'. In 2018, Yuriy (figure 17) was awarded the Taras Shevchenko National Prize for his cinematographic work. During the social and cultural revolution in Ukraine (2013-2015) he directed and shotthe documentary web-series 'Babylon 13'. He was injured filming the protests in Kyiv, where he also documented the first two deaths of Euromaidan protestors. While filming events in Crimea, he was abducted by Russian Special Forces and held captive for six days.

Figure 17. Yuriy Gruzinov. (Photo credit: G. Ercolani, 2019)

'Babylon 13' is a cinematography collective which documents the crisis in Ukraine (Kyiv, Crimea, and currently in Eastern and Southern Ukraine). The short films comprising this cinematographic creation, include 'First Death', about the first protestor killed on the Maidan; 'Heavenly Hundred', about the dozens of other protesters killed during the last days of the protests; 'Prolog', which was filmed following the first clash between protesters and the Berkut in late November; 'Mediator', about a priest who stood between the protesters and riot police in an attempt to prevent violence; 'The Firewood Revolution', about a group of protesters, who guarded the barricades on Institutskaya Street; 'Cultural Checkpoint', about the social relations that developed among protesters on the Maidan; and 'Solo', about a fighter who participated in the riots on Hrushevskoho Street. The documentaries are voiceless, and represent the individual narratives of seven heroes of Maidan. Yuriy's technique makes the documentary unique and revealing of hidden truths: 'I shoot my documentary from both sides (the police side and the demonstrators' side). The police covered their face in order to not to be recognized, the demonstrators only to protect themselves. A lot of police did not agree with the official policy but they had to obey'. Nevertheless, Yuriy, adds in his documentary, an element of hope which comes out the Manichean struggle: 'the symbol of the baby born with blood ..... This new born baby represents New Ukraine, and he is ready to kill the new dictator. What is important, then, is what this baby will become'.

However, the work of Oles Kromplias, activist, volunteer, photographer and war correspondent, adds a couple of important elements to the concept of Maidan as a place where the struggle between good and evil took place. His project 'The War is Close' (figure 18, 19), co-produced with the Maidan Museum, is part of an information warfare campaign, in which Oles want us to feel anxiety, to live the sense of war that is within us. A total of twenty silhouettes of people shot with bullets—both soldiers and civilians, and even children—were located in 2018 on the streets of the capital (Kyiv) in places where, according to Kromplias, people were not ready to see them. Oles clearly explained his project, its meaning, and the message he wanted to transmit: 'in my work with the sculptures, which are human-size metal shapes pierced by bullets, I work on my emotional approach. Some of these sculptures are present in the National Museum of the History of Ukraine. And as an artistic project they were distributed around the city of Kyiv. What is good is that you can touch these sculptures, you can feel them. Basically, the meaning of the project "The war is nearby" means that you can feel the war, people can understand that the holes in the metal shapes were made using real bullets. These sculptures provoke anxiety. It is very important for me to work with emotions, fear, stress, anxiety. My mission is not to sell my work. About my sculptures, I work on a project in which the sculptures have the shape of soldiers, and I expose them together with the sounds of combat area. And this experiment was very painful to me and to other people. Some people escaped from the show room. My sculptures transmit to you emotion because you can touch them. This is the reason I made those holes (made with firing real bullets), because you can touch them and they give you the sensation of what it means to touch a hole made by a bullet. Talking about reaction of people toward my sculptures, I have one very interesting experience. I had some of my sculptures exhibited in a park in Kyiv. One day I was riding my bike and I wanted to see my sculptures, and I wanted to see if they were ok. And I found a sculpture with a bandage, like someone wanted to cure the sculpture. Differently, other people made graffiti on my sculptures and I had to clean them'.

Oles enlarges the psychological perception of Maidan and adds an emotional element which is original and extremely important for all the artistic production of Maidan: the imminence that something dramatic was going to happen. The anxiety of imminence was the sensation lived by the protestors during the Maidan events, to be under the scrutiny of hidden snipers ready to fire at them, as dramatically demonstrated by the killing of the Heavenly Hundred.

For Garcia Canclini 'art is the place of imminence — the place where we catch sight of things that are just at the point of occurring. Art gains its attraction in part from the fact that it proclaims something that could happen, promising meaning or modifying meaning through insinuations. (...) By saying that art is situated in imminence, I am postulating a possible relationship with "the real" that is as oblique or indirect as that in music or abstract painting. Works of art do not merely "suspend" reality; they situate themselves in a prior moment, when the real is possible, when it has not yet broken down. They treat facts as events that are about to come into being' (Garcia Canclini, 2014: xiii-xiv).

However, imminence is an essential element in Maidan as a spiritual place because it recalls the fact that we are experiencing a sacral-sacred experience-events in which the artist performs his/her mission as shaman, healers, initiator, and prophet which transform the audience-people. Oles wants his work to be perceived as an art work which provokes emotions like consciousness: 'Through my art (photos and sculptures) I want that people change to the better. The people can change and they can change the situations. People are growing and they change the way they think. I want to make people more conscious about what is happening around the world and talk about personal responsibility. People must think that they are responsible for the political situation, because they voted a specific politician. If some of the elected politicians do something bad, I should feel guilty for it, because we voted him'.

Figure 18. 'The war is nearby', courtesy of OlesKromplias

Figure 19. 'The war is nearby', courtesy of OlesKromplias

Maidan as an anthropological place: Marc Augé (2011: 158) defines an anthropological place as 'a place intensely symbolized, lived by individuals in which they found their spatial, temporal, individual and collective benchmarks. For the anthropologist, at the same time, it is a space in which he or she can read, and decode the social relations and the common forms of belonging'.

This means that the reality of Maidan is constituted by the 'symbolic universe' that the social scientist must understand and deconstruct. For Berger and Luckmann: 'the symbolic universe is conceived as the matrix of all socially objectivated and subjectively real meaning; the entire historic society and the entire biography of the individual are seen as events taking place within this universe. Of particular import is that the marginal situations of the life of the individual (marginal, that is, in not being included in the reality of everyday existence in society) are also compassed in the symbolic universe (…) Within the symbolic universe these detached realms of reality are integrated within a meaningful totality that "explains", perhaps also justifies them. (…) The symbolic universe is, of course, constructed by means of social objectivations. (…) That is, symbolic universes are social products with history. If one is to understand their meaning, one has to understand the history of their production. (...) The symbolic universe provides order for the subjective apprehension of the biographical experience. Experiences belonging to different spheres of reality are integrated by incorporation in the same, overarching universe of meaning. (...) This integration of the realities of marginal situation within the paramount reality of everyday live is of great importance, because these situations constitute the most acute threat to taken-for-granted, routinized existence in society' (Berger and Luckmann, 1991: 114-116).

And this is what happens to the practice of everyday life of people who come across the Maidan square. The anthropological place is a symbolic universe, which always recalls and refers to Maidan as a myth, a spiritual place, and a bloody struggle for dignity.

The following picture shows how the whole area of Maidan speaks of the Maidan events and its martyrs.

Here, permanent installations by the Maidan Museum in the center of Maidan Square tell the story of the Maidan events (in Ukrainian and in English) (figure 20).

Figure 20. Maidan. (Photo credit: G. Ercolani 2019)

Around the area of Maidan, interventions in public spaces point to the martyrs of Maidan, the 'Heavenly Hundred', and these places form memorials which are visited by people who remember their sacrifice. And every year, on February 20, there are celebrations to commemorate the day of the Heavenly Hundred Heroes, which can be and are interpreted as collective representations. The official, yearly Memorial Day of the Heavenly Hundred Heroes, February 20, was established by Decree of the President of Ukraine on February 11, 2015. All these contribute to the sacredness of the place and of the myth of Maidan (figure 21, 22, 23, 24, 25).

Figure 21. In memory of the Heroes of the Heavenly Hundred.
(Photo credit: G. Ercolani, 2019)

Figure 22. In memory of the Heroes of the Heavenly Hundred.
(Photo credit: G. Ercolani, 2019)

Figure 23. In memory of the Heroes of the Heavenly Hundred.
(Photo credit: G. Ercolani, 2019)

Figure 24. In memory of the Heroes of the Heavenly Hundred.
(Photo credit: G. Ercolani, 2019)

Figure 25. In memory of the Heroes of the Heavenly Hundred.
(Photo credit: G. Ercolani, 2019)

Maidan as an emotional field: the whole of the Maidan experience is enveloped with emotions, and strong emotions are implicated in social identity. Maidan is the field of research, an emotional field in which words, myths, symbols, rituals, memories, histories, personal experiences are all mixed with personal emotions. And Maidan is about the construction of a new identity. This identity, to draw on Fukuyama (2018: 131), is rooted in 'thymos' (the part of the soul that craves recognition of dignity) experienced emotionally through feelings of pride, shame, and anger. As has already been suggested, it is important that the researcher feels the emotions of the 'field' in order to understand it, and every emotion tells a story and has an historical dimension. This point is well expressed by Beatty, for whom 'the difficulties of recognizing and interpreting emotional episodes in the field open onto general problems of method; and they mask deeper questions about the nature of emotion and the coherence of the emotion concept. (...) Mistake the emotion and you mistake the scene; misread the scene and you confound the disposition of the actors; get that wrong and you bungle the whole story. (...) The ability to recognize and comprehend emotion affects the quality of our engagement with others, the sense we make of experience, and the life that goes into our ethnography. For the anthropologist the problem of what constitutes emotion begins and ends in the field' (Beatty, 2019: 15). Emotions do have a specific importance in this work because they are tied to the production and reception of artefacts which constantly remind and point to the Maidan. As an emotional field, Maidan lives within the artefacts collected and in the activities of the Maidan Museum: 'these objects are not only seen, but also experienced multi-sensorially' (Svasek, 2012: 11).

Therefore, it is necessary to 'feel' Maidan: in this emotional field 'artefacts can be active triggers and mediators of a wide variety of emotions, defined as interactive, partly mental, partly physical processes which undermine rigid theoretical distinctions between "mind" and "body", "the individual" and "the social", and "intrapsychic realms" and "extrapsychic, external worlds". Equally, it is important to recognize emotions which engage the viewers or audience for Maidan if one is to make sense of its transmission. Emotions are regarded as experiential and interpretational processes in which individuals actively relate to their human and non-human environments through discursive practices and embodied experience. These dynamics are intersubjective because individual beings influence each other's dispositions, generating new meanings and feelings as they live their social lives' (Svasek, 2007: 67).

Maidan's artefacts embody the Maidan events and, as drawing on Svasek's argument (2007: 82), they cause direct emotional engagement. Such experiential effects cannot be understood by formal, stylistic or semiotic analyses of a visual imaginary (see also Bleiker, 2018) because they deny some of the most fundamentally spontaneous elements of the relations between feeling and perception. Those emotional responses to images are, at least to some extent, conditioned by socio-spatial contexts. Thus, for Svasek (2012: 8-13), emotional processes are at least partially culturally constituted, informed by situated social practices. Drawing on her understanding helps one to make sense of the intense combination of emotional narrating and reasoned explanation that is captured in Maidan.

Oleksandr Ivanovych Melnyk, in his account of his Maidan experience, unfolds and puts together these concepts of emotions and identity. For him, Maidan, more than a ritual, embodied: 'a feeling of solidarity that people had each other, people came together and they felt it. I went to the Maidan Revolutions: (1) the Orange Revolution; and (2) the Revolution of Dignity. I cannot say that I changed after Maidan, but this was because since I was a child, I saw how the Soviet regime was unfair, and my family suffered during the Soviet time, but I was sure that everything was going to change'. And he recalls his school time 'during my childhood, I went to school and there everybody was speaking Russian, and only few people spoke Ukrainian. During my childhood, I saw a lot of burden on the Ukrainian speaking part of Ukraine, and I had doubt that this part of the Country was going to survive. In the 60s, in the cities, we had appraisal of artists, and this is when I started talking about freedom. And when I was listening to different opinions, I understood that Ukraine was not going to be destroyed. In my school time (9th grade) I was the only boy in my classroom to speak Ukrainian. When I started studying at the Art Academy, there were students coming from different part of Ukraine, and there was a small group of people speaking Ukrainian. However, when I took part to the two Maidan revolutions, I realized that there were millions of people speaking Ukrainian. After, I organized an exhibition. While at Maidan, I was a participant; at the same time, I wanted to record the event. I never experienced so much happiness as the one the people were expressing in Maidan (Orange and Dignity revolutions). I know that is very difficult for people to change, therefore, I do not see Maidan as a Revolution, but as an evolution. In January 2014, I organized a Biennale exhibition in order to celebrate Taras Shevchenko, the national Ukrainian poet. My purpose was to teach people about national history, culture, and how to change society'.

For Sasha Komyakhov (artist, freelance illustrator) emotions represent his participation in Maidan: 'Maidan started with students but when we saw the students bitten by the police, we joined them to support them. It is like when you were at school, you saw your friends in need of help and you join them. During the Maidan event I was a photographer, and my main idea was to document the events. I have a lot of pictures of the event. I tried to avoid fire but I was injured. I am from Kyiv and I joined the Maidan basically from the beginning and I was there always, and during the night I was going back to my place. The Spirit of Maidan is still present, and you can see it because after the Maidan events people start volunteering association and so on, something that before Maidan never existed in Ukraine'.

Maryna Sochenko's canvases talk about emotions, stress, tension, violence and identity-recognition: 'I was always in Maidan, since the beginning. There, I started to teach people how to draw and to paint and I made hundreds of portraits. The reason behind me doing the portraits is that a lot of people thought that the persons who were gathering and protesting in Maidan were homeless. But I knew some of these persons; therefore, I decided to start doing portraits about them in order to show that they were not homeless. On the portraits I did, I wrote on them the name of the person, his/her origin (where he/she was coming from), and the date of the portrait. I have portraits of people from the beginning to the end of Maidan revolution. I was painting them in Maidan, they were posing in front of me, it was very cold, I was freezing. At the end I was portraying people from all over Ukraine. In a way It was a kind of art therapy, because for them, for these people, it was extremely important to be acknowledged that they were important for the revolution. People were under tension and stress, but when they posed for the portrait they relaxed, and talked. I did a couple of exhibitions but the BERKUT smashed everything. When I was doing my exhibition in the House of the Trade Unions, the employers of the House told me that they were not responsible for our works because there was the threat that the BERKUT would come and destroy everything; however, the protestors came and they said that they were protecting the works of art and us. For people it was extremely important to see these portraits of Maidan in the House of the Trade Unions as well in other locations'.

Figure 26. Maryna Sochenko in her studio. (Photo credit: G. Ercolani, 2019)

Yuriy Gruzinov identifies how the emotions produced in Maidan were the same as those present in the conflict area of Donbass: 'after the Maidan protests a lot of Maidan people went to Donbass to fight. The most important is that Ukrainians did not start a war against Ukrainians. As the domestic situation was changing in

Ukraine (new president, etc.) the people of Maidan started to understand that their presence was not needed in Maidan anymore and went to Donbass where the enemy was. The first volunteers to Donbass were coming from Maidan. And the emotions of the people in Donbass were the same as the emotions of the people in Maidan. They felt the same energy (Donbass and Maidan). And the war did not end in Maidan and in Donbass. Maidan is a never-ending protest in the name of dignity. Maidan is a protest mind set. The Spirit of Maidan is still living in the soul of the people. Maidan is not finished; Maidan is inside the head of the people. However, the people who have Maidan in their mind they do nothing, because right now they think about the future of their kids and they think that the future of their kids is safe. Society is very calm, permanent group, and it is very difficult to have it to move. During these five years people is tired of war. But is like fire beneath the ashes. People look calm, but if the government/politics will create a problem, the society will react. Now, after six years, Ukraine is changed, is like Israel, meaning that everybody has a weapon in their house. Maidan is like a rite of passage; you cross a line and you change'.

Hence, emotions point to discourses, and discourses of emotions and emotivity produce knowledge about self and society that may create, maintain or challenge power relations and thus influence subjectivity. Discourses of emotions are often played through emotional practices that can have strong performative dimension. And emotions are embodied experiences in which the emotional field (Maidan) is apprehended through multisensorial engagement.

Maidan as a chosen trauma: Serhii Plokhy (2015) recalls the experience of Bohdan Solchanyk. A twenty-eight year old historian, sociologist, and budding poet who taught at the Ukrainian Catholic University in Lviv, he came to Kyiv from Lviv by train in the morning of February 20, 2014 to join the Revolution. This very new revolution, in which hundreds of thousands of people were pouring into the street of downtown Kyiv 'to demand reform, the end of government corruption, and closer ties with the European Union. Solchanyk felt that his place was among the protesters in

Kyiv. February 20 marked his fourth foray into the revolution, which turned out to be his last. A few hours after his arrival in Kyiv, sniper fire killed Solchanyk along with dozens of other protestors. In death, he would become one of the "Heavenly Hundred" – those more than one hundred protesters killed in Kyiv in January and February 2014. Those killings ended twenty-two years of generally nonviolent politics in Ukraine and turned a dramatic page in its history. The democracy peacefully acquired in the final days of the Soviet Union and the independence won at the ballot box in December 1991 would now require defense not only with words and marches but also with arms' (Plokhy, 2015: 337).

The playwright Neda Nedjana recalls the trauma of the night of Feb 18-19, 2014, in which the new Ukraine was born: 'I was in the metro, people were singing Christmas songs, and in that precise moment I said "NO" and I decided to continue my protest for the future generation. 18-19Feb 2014 was the bloody night. This was a night of catharsis; this was the night of the big change. In that precise night the New Ukraine was born. This night represents the founding/origin myth of New Ukraine. In Maidan there was a rhythm, a pulse. I remember people started singing the national anthem and they started crying. Before that night (18-19 Feb 2014), people were living in the myth of Maidan, after that night a New Ukraine was founded. That night represents a rite of passage, of catharsis, a miracle, all the people who lived that experience have changed. At the same time, it was a revolution that has employed internet. I could be impossible to have the Maidan revolution without internet and Facebook. The revolution of dignity was about: (1) the defence of dignity: (2) how everyone of us can contribute to the society; (3) what can I do for the others? Therefore, Maidan as a Myth, represents: (1) New Ukraine; (2) A new way of thinking. Maidan was for (1) Europe; and (2) for dignity. Ukrainian language definitely became the "official" language of the revolution'.

Maidan and the sacrifice of the 'Heavenly Hundred' represents the traumatic event, the chosen trauma, in which a large group identity is forged. Here, chosen trauma means 'the collective mental representation of an event that has caused a large group to face drastic common losses, to feel helpless and victimized by another group, and to share a humiliating injury' (Volkan, 2004: 48). But it is a chosen trauma, a choice against an alternative of mere submission, and a choice to embrace a hard path to some hope of liberation, as if one were accepting the amputation of diseased fingers to save the whole arm.

Vamik Volkan (2004: 37), in his work dedicated to large group identity, identifies 'chosen traumas' as one of the seven 'threads' that, when woven together, compose large-group identity. These comprise shared, tangible reservoirs for images associated with positive emotion; shared 'good' identifications; absorption of 'others' bad qualities; absorption of [revolutionary or transforming] leaders' internal worlds; chosen glories; chosen traumas; formation of symbols that develop their own autonomy. The concept of 'large-group identity' has a correlation with the Spirit of Maidan, the homo Maidan, and the Revolution of Dignity, and introduces the theory of Maidan as a chosen trauma. Maidan represents in this view a collective shared transformation.

The concept of large group-identity, according to Volkan (2004: 11-13), describes 'how thousands of individuals, most of whom will never meet in their life-times, are bound by an intense sense of sameness by belonging to the same ethnic, religious, national, or ideological group. (…) Our relationship with our large-group identity, in ordinary times is like breathing. We breathe constantly, and we are unaware of it unless someone reminds us of the fact that we need air to survive. (…) If our large-group identity is under attack, we behave like an individual with pneumonia or in a burning building; we are acutely aware of our large-group affiliation, its perceived characteristics, our emotional investment in it, and how we are "similar" to thousands or millions of others who also belong to the large group. At the same time, we separate ourselves from those we consider different from us. Under such circumstances, we see how our individual sense of the self, our personal identity, becomes entwined with our large-group identity. (…) Threats to the abstract psychological creation that is large-group identity produce shared anxiety, and this may lead to societal regression among the members of the large group. In general terms, regression is an individual involves a return to some of the psychological expectations, wishes, fears, and associated mental defense mechanism of an earlier stage of human development. (...) Large groups also regress. Activities such as rallying around the leader, exhibiting flags, attempting to "purify" the group from those whose names or skin colors suggest that they may be affiliated with the enemy, and dividing the world into clashing civilizations may be related to concepts as patriotism and national security. (...) A group's realistic efforts to feel secure merge with expressions of human nature under stress, and, in certain areas, reality and fantasy become blurred'. In this identity process of large group identity such as the case of the Ukrainian protestors, Maidan does play an important role in the fabrication of their own identity. It forms an acculturation process, and is transformative in the transmission, through art, literature, documentary, music and other cultural practices, of the experience of the traumatic event. In this way it transforms a traumatic experience into the centre of collective identification.

However, for Volkan (1999: 46), a chosen trauma is 'more than a simple recollection; it is a shared mental representation of the event, which includes realistic information, fantasized expectations, intense feelings and defenses against unacceptable thoughts. The art of Maidan embodies all the above, and it is an art which has transformed horrific events into something beautiful (e.g. Tatyana Cheprasova's work discussed earlier). Thus, to be able to understand how past suffering can gain social and political significance, Svasek suggests that 'it is necessary also to examine the process of social and bodily interaction and sensual perceptual experience' (Svasek, 2005: 196). And Maidan was a trauma which involved social and bodily interaction, sensual perceptual experience, and a dialectical space between individuality and sociality.

Everything presented so far in this argument constitutes the genealogy, the archaeology and the pillars of the culture of Maidan, where the notion of 'culture' draws on Geertz's conception: culture 'denotes an historically transmitted pattern of meanings embodied in symbols, a system of inherited conceptions expressed in symbolic forms by means of which men communicate, perpetuate, and develop their knowledge about and attitudes toward life' (Geertz, 1973: 89). Similarly, for Bouchard, culture 'refers to the more or less structured and coherent universe the symbols of which nurture the members of a collectivity and govern social interactions' (Bouchard, 2017: 4).

And in this culture and symbolic universe of Maidan, art plays an important role. Because myth, and, one might add, spiritual-anthropological elements, come into being through 'powerful representations that express the most profound feelings of a society, that nurture identities and ideologies, that structure a vision of the past and the future, and that inspire collective and circumscribe public debates' (Bouchard, 2017: 3).

3.3. The Symbols of Maidan: Art, Identity and the Spirit of Maidan

This sub-section respects Gombrich's view that 'there really is no such thing as art; there are only artists' (Gombrich, 1994: 4). And 'art' is conceived with reference to the academic work, Moussienko's 'Art of Maidan' (2016), as well as to the objects and art creations, which are part of the Museum of Maidan. It follows from this view that the focus is on the artists' creative process. The art of Maidan ('the creative force of freedom'), carries an aura (Benjamin, 1973; Peters, 2020; Freeland, 2001; Dal Lago and Giordano, 2006) and is considered 'conceptual art' (concept: Maidan myth which carries an ideology; Harris, 2008: 60-63). The artists produced the 'symbols of Maidan', which are part of the imaginary, the symbolic universe of Maidan, they embody the Spirit of Maidan, and they are essential elements in the manufacturing of 'antagonist' collective imaginaries (Bouchard, 2017), in the Maidan mythification process (Bouchard, 2017), in the social process of identity formation (Jenkins, 2014), and in the establishment of the strong relation between identity-identification-interpellation (Althusser, 1988; Ranciere, 2014).

It must be stressed, however, that the umbrella term of 'the art of Maidan' covers all the objects, artefacts and other items which now are part of the Maidan Museum. These objects carry an aura because 'the aura is the unrepeatable essence of a work reaches its status thanks to a ritual-event of a creative subject' (Peters, 2020: 74) and 'we define the aura as the set of social and cognitive frameworks that make art what it is' (Dal Lago and Giordano, 2006: 16). However, the aura for Benjamin has its roots in the authenticity of the object, the artefact has an aura because authentically belong to the Maidan Revolution and 'the uniqueness of a work of art is inseparable from its being imbedded in the fabric of tradition. (...) Originally the contextual integration of art in tradition found its expression in the cult. We know that the earliest art works originated in the service of a ritual—first the magical, then the religious kind. It is significant that the existence of the work of art with reference to its aura is never entirely separated from its ritual function. In other words, the unique value of the "authentic" work of art has its basis in ritual, the location of its original use value. This ritualistic basis, however remote, is still recognizable as secularized ritual even in the most profane forms of cult of beauty' (Benjamin, 1973: 225-226).

The Maidan revolution—with its rituals and martyrs—is the ritual-event from which were created the works of art, as well as the social and cognitive framework, which define them as object of art. This means that the 'symbols of Maidan' must be read inside the social myths and collective imaginaries paradigm developed by Bouchard (2017); however, they must be considered as antagonistic to the official ones anchored in a static post-soviet past-as indeed most were intended to be. The phenomenon of the social myth of Maidan must also be situated inside the universe of sacredness and collective imaginaries (vehicle-message). As a result, the 'symbols of Maidan' found their real meaning once they are fully collocated inside the category of myth-sacredness and collective imaginaries-vehicle-message.

The interviews allowed the collection of information about the 'symbols of Maidan'. Being semi-structured, they allowed each respondent to open up around their ideas and understanding of three main points, namely the participation of the artist in Maidan, the artistic creative-inspirational process, and the production of the 'symbols of Maidan'.

As result, the research was able to identify the symbols and archetypes of Maidan. These embody, summarize, condense, and speak for the whole experience and interpretation of the Maidan events as lived by the informants-interviewees. They become icons carrying the message of the Revolution of Dignity, and connecting it to both religious and secular icons of the past. They speak of death and hope, representing the Spirit of Maidan, and epitomize spatial, temporal, individual and collective benchmarks; and they constitute the aesthetic language of Maidan, which survives the end of the Revolution.

As Bouchard argues, 'myth is presented as a sacralised ethos expressed in symbols' (Bouchard, 2017: 86). Here one can see how those myths and that ethos take concrete forms in the material curated in the Museum.

According to the artists interviewed, and as recorded in the interview material presented here, the following are the symbols of Maidan, which represent the archetypes and the Spirit of Maidan:

1. Yolka (Christmas tree).
2. Tyres (burned tyres).
3. Helmets (reinterpreted painted helmets).
4. Shields (reinterpreted painted shields).
5. Fire barrels and tents.
6. Molotov cocktails.
7. Tryzub (trident — the state coat of arms of Ukraine).
8. Blue-Yellow colors (National colors of Ukraine).
9. Saint Michael the Archangel (Saint Patron of the city of Kyiv).
10. Religious images/symbols.
11. Fire.
12. Taras Shevchenko (National poet of Ukraine).
13. Cossack 'Mamai' with 'bandura' (the hero who goes around the world and helps people).
14. Cossack's hair style (khokhol-oseledets).
15. Ukrainian Cossack camp in the 17th century (Euromaidan square).

16. Malevich's 'Black square'.

In the discussion which follows, the author explores and explains each of these key symbols and gives illustrations of how they inform the Spirit of Maidan, as well as discussing how they interact together to form the warp and weft of the fabric of that spirit.

The project 'stamps for Maidan' by Yulia Ovcharenko summarizes and visualizes most of the above-mentioned symbols of Maidan (figures 27, 28, 29, 30, 31, 32, 33). Stamps for Maidan, is a real example of artistic objects (art by intention) created with a specific use, like the one to serve in a post service (art by metamorphosis) and to facilitate communication among the Maidan protesters. The genealogy of this project through the eyes of Yulia, carries the whole of the Maidan experience. She explains: 'the aim of the Maidan Mail Service was to help contacts among the protesters in Maidan. All the protesters were living in tents in Maidan Square. And I wanted them to become friends. Therefore, I took some plastic boxes which I converted in mail boxes and I placed them in the tent city in Maidan, in front of every tent, and people started do write letters to other people who were in other tents. Every tent had a special mail code (like a post code). And we established a table like a post office and people were coming to us and posted letters to people to different tents using the tent post codes. Unfortunately, this mail service did not last too long because it was smashed when the Ukrainian House was occupied by the Ukrainian police (BERKUT). However, in March 2014 we started to promote this Maidan Mail Service again. We put a table in front of the post office again and the protestors who wanted to write letters to their family were provided with free envelop and stamps. Even if we are in an electronic era, we wanted to fabricate some artefact to push people to write letter. Now, these letters are written prove of the events of Maidan. So, the mail service started and we produced stamps. They were free, but you had to make something good for the others in exchange. You did something good for the protesters and you received stamps. This is because in Maidan there was a lot of people who were volunteering and they were working for free (they prepared food and distributed it completely free, etc.). Then, after Sep 1st, 2015, we decided to make stamps in a very artistic way. And on these stamps we reproduced the symbols of Maidan. However, even if by that date Maidan was ended, the main idea behind this initiative was to continue to promote the Spirit of Maidan and to preserve the memory of the Maidan events. For me it was very important to work on these stamps because I was very moved and shacked by the events and I was able to reproduce the symbols of Maidan on the stamps.'

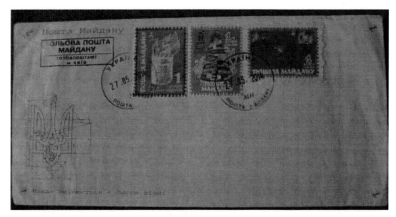

Figure 27. Maidan stamps, courtesy of Yulia Ovcharenko.

Figure 28. Maidan stamps, courtesy of Yulia Ovcharenko.

Figure 29. Maidan Stamps, courtesy of Yulia Ovcharenko.

Figure 30. Maidan stamps, courtesy of Yulia Ovcharenko.

Figure 31. Maidan stamps, courtesy of Yulia Ovcharenko.

Figure 32. Maidan stamps, courtesy of Yulia Ovcharenko.

Figure 33. Maidan stamps, courtesy of Yulia Ovcharenko.

As argued by Joy Hendry 'symbolism pervades human behaviour, at even the most mundane levels, and the ability to use symbols, including speech, is one of the ways in which the behaviour of humans is said to be distinguished from the behaviour of other animals. (...) Symbols in any society must be used in a systematic way, or the members would feel lost, just as the outsider feels lost on a first exposure to the society. In fact, it would not be going too far to describe the whole concept of society as a set of shared symbols' (Hendry, 1999: 82-83). What these symbols also do is reach back to connect the sensibility of Maidan with recognizable religious and secular representations which capture imaginaries from Ukraine's past which are meaningful both to their creators and to Ukrainian visitors or viewers online.

However, it is necessary to find a definition of symbol and to anchor our symbols of Maidan in it. According to the Concise Oxford English Dictionary (2011 ed.), a 'symbol' is defined as: '1. a mark or character used in conventional representation of something, e.g. a letter standing for a chemical element or a character in musical notation. 2. a thing that represents or stands for something else, especially a material object representing something abstract. (...)'. This general definition requires a more specific identification in the use of the term in an anthropological or ethnographic study. For Geertz (1973: 91) symbols 'are tangible formulations of notions, abstractions from experience fixed in perceptible forms, concrete embodiments of ideas, attitudes, judgments, longings, or beliefs'. And Womack highlights the importance and the presence of symbols in our daily life. For her 'no one can escape the power of symbols. If we are not involved in the symbolic complexes of religion and magic, we observe symbolic dramas on television, at the movies, or on the sporting field. If we manage to evade the influence of symbols in our daily lives — which is virtually impossible — we will still encounter symbols in our dreams. Wherever we look, our world is "peopled" with gods, heroes, and demons who act out our hopes, fears, conflicts, and triumphs on the large screen of mass media or on the small screen of our dreams. Symbols are the language of religion, magic, and expressive culture, including art, literature, theatre, music, festivals, and sporting events. (...) Symbols are, above all, a means of communication. In general terms, symbols are images, words, or behaviors that have multiple levels of meaning. Symbols stand for concepts that are too complex to be stated directly in words' (Womack, 2005: 1-2).

However, according to Álvarez Munárriz (2015: 312), the symbolic universe has to be understood as a memory or a depository where, in a conscious or unconscious way, we refer and draw in order to orient and legitimize our behaviour. Therefore, it is a key category in explaining human actions and phenomenon. And for Lisón Tolosana (2014: 238-240), symbols are catalysts of emotions in which the symbols and their respective signs interact each other. The symbol works as a *passepartout* category in ordinary language because everything can be transformed into a symbol and it acts in an environment of metaphors and through corresponding analogies (the symbol appeals). Whilst the sign develops in a homonymous milieu, it is less vague and more precise and concrete.

Cassirer (1972) links the survival of humankind in his own environment to his capacity to create symbols: 'every organism, even the lowest, is not only in a vague sense adapted to but entirely fitted into its environment. According to its anatomical structure it possesses a certain *Mewrknetz* and a certain *Wirknetz* – a receptor system and an effector system. Without the cooperation and equilibrium of these two systems the organism could not survive. The receptor system by which a biological species receives outward stimuli and the effector system by which it reacts to them are in all cases closely interwoven. (…) (However,) man has discovered a new method of adapting himself to his environment. Between the receptor system and the effector system, which are to be found in all animal species, we find in man a third link which we may describe as the *symbolic system*. This new acquisition transforms the whole of human life. As compared with other animals, man lives not merely in a broader reality; he leaves, so to speak, in a new *dimension* of reality. (…) No longer in a merely physical universe, man lives in a symbolic universe. Language, myth, art, and religion are parts of this universe. They are the varied threads which weave the symbolic net, the tangled web of human experience. All human progress in thought and experience refines upon and strengthens this net. No longer can man confront reality immediately; he cannot see it, as it were, face to face. Physical reality seems to recede in proportion as man's symbolic activity advances. Instead of dealing with the things themselves man is in a sense constantly conversing with himself. He has enveloped himself in linguistic forms, in artistic images, in mythical symbols or religious rites that he cannot see or know anything except by the interposition of this artificial medium. His situation is the same in the theoretical as in the practical sphere. Even here man does not live in a world of hard facts, or according to his immediate needs and desires. He lives rather in the midst of imaginary emotions, in hopes and fears, in illusions and disillusions, in his fantasies and dreams. (…) Hence, instead of defining man as an animal rationale, we should define him as an *animal symbolicum*' (Cassirer, 1972: 24-26).

And these symbols are shared by the Ukrainian society: they are deeply internalized, form part of the national identity, and they evoke strong feelings for Ukrainian people. Adopting the link between symbol and emotions provided by Lisón Tolosana (2014:

238-240), which establishes symbols as catalysts of emotions, I would want to argue that these symbols can 'be called sites of the super-consciousness — namely, the first references that lie at the core of every culture and that have a very strong hold on society given that they possess an authority akin to sacredness. Belonging more to emotion than to reason, these references also permeate the minds of individuals, touch them deep inside, and motivate their choices, either by mobilizing them, by sending them forth in pursuit of bold plans, or on the contrary by inhibiting them' (Bouchard, 2017: 8).

These symbols were already present in the collective imaginaries of the Ukrainian people, but through the Maidan they have acquired new meaning and a new life. Now, in their new meaning and signification, they represent the Spirit of Maidan, they carry the antagonist message of the Revolution of Dignity, and they strongly reaffirm the purpose of the struggle, the fight for dignity, the state or quality of being worthy of honour or respect.

Art in Maidan was a clear act of artivism, it was about creating symbols and an aesthetic of imminence; it was embedded in the protest and was the result of revolutionary creativity. *Artivism* here is a term that indicates the union between art and political activism, a combination that has a long history (with particular characteristics in former communist countries), but which has only been defined more recently, in relation to the appearance of the first telematic networks in the 1980s. It then spread with the development of the internet, social media and digital culture. As a practice that is configured through the actions of artists and collectives, characterised by a strong vocation for social and political commitment (Bazzichelli, 2006: 2013), artivism crosses different fields of expression — performance, street art, video art, net art, subvertising, guerrilla marketing — and uses media languages and formats from an antagonistic, critical and counter-information perspective.

For Milohnić artivism is a kind of 'interventionism', which uses 'cultural-manifestation techniques in order to become constituted in the field of the political' (Milohnić, 2005: 4). Furthermore, 'the transversality of these practices and their hybrid nature enable quick passages from the predominantly artistic into the predominantly political sphere and back' (Milohnić, 2005:12). The process which created Maidan and maintains its spirit is a very apposite illustration of this interchange between practices, and the dialogue which it sustains produces highly original work, some of which is cited or illustrated throughout this book.

Kozak (2017), in his paper 'Art Embedded into Protest: Staging Ukrainian Maidan', follows the events and focuses 'on the interaction between an occupation and the artworks, embedded into its environment, as a dynamic system of semantic interdependence similar to the hermeneutic circle in which the whole and its parts might be interpreted only through mutual references. In other words, one could argue not only that an occupation serves as a platform for artworks, but also that through a dynamism of events it constructs and displaces their meaning, while artworks, respectively, not only reflect but also shape the occupation's identity and thus indirectly orchestrate a dynamism of events' (Kozak, 2017: 10). Kozak does not list the symbols of Maidan – see the list suggested above, which identifies some of the most important symbols, but which is not exhaustive. But his work is about the relation between artists, extemporary artists, their artworks; it explains the chronology of the Maidan events and pre-existing public space. These pre-existing public spaces reflected the 'malformed nature of the post-Soviet state system, deeply rooted in its dark colonial past and somehow camouflaged with the rhetoric of the "national rebirth"' (Kozak, 2017: 15). At the same time Kozak doubts whether we should label such objects as artworks, 'to escape this slippery terminological trap, I will adopt the approach Amy Mullin (2003: 191) used to justify the notion of activist art. She borrowed the term from Lippard to define a kind of art that was not just politically "concerned" but politically "involved", which implies a political action and "actively seeks public participation" both in the process of its creation and in its perception' (Kozak, 2017: 23).

That revolutionary creativity is analysed by Moussienko in her work 'Art of Maidan' (2016). Moussienko underlines the fact that 'the artistic factor has always been constitutive for Ukraine, where passionate political activities have often been recruited from among the country's artists. During a long historical period in which Ukrainians did not have their own state, they had both creative artists and politicians as their spiritual leaders. This phenomenon may be described with the words of the Ukrainian poet, Yevhen Malaniuk: "If a nation does not have leaders, poets are its leaders". In a similar vein, the English radical poet Shelley asserted that poets were 'the unacknowledged legislators of mankind', above all in the face of tyrannical state power. Artists not only preserved the nation, but they also raised it, taught it, and created it. It's no coincidence that seventeenth century Cossack Hetman Ivan Mazepa was a composer, and that Western Ukraine's socialist movement stems from the vastly admired poet and writer Ivan Franko (who unsuccessfully ran for office several times). As the Cossack state decayed, Ukrainians created a state through their art.(...) Richard Wagner, in his work "Art and Revolution", underlined that art could sanctify a revolution and give it real beauty, a sacred beauty, as art holds a special place in the Ukrainian revolutionary events of 2013-2014. Detailed analysis of rich empirical material gathered by the author certifies that at the Maidan, there were different kinds and genres of art: performance, installation, cinema, music, painting, sculpture, and literature, the full extent of the creative artistic pallet. Professionals and amateurs, famous artists and artistic youth: the Maidan united them all and became a great artistic work in itself, an ultimate installation' (see also Moussienko, 2016: 11). Moussienko lists the creativity of Maidan, which employed poster art, photography, sculpture, painting, art associations, cinema, and music. However, she adds, 'a special note should be made of numerous performances on a yellow-and-blue piano that first appeared near the Presidential Administration building, where a musician played for police forces. The piano then moved to the Kyiv City Council building, and eventually arrived at the barricades on Hrushevskoko. A community of gifted pianists played the piano, "the instrument of freedom", as it came to be known, wearing balaclavas. Activists in Lviv, Donetsk, Uzhhorod, Kirovohrad, and other regional centres followed the Kyiv example, and yellow-and-blue pianos appeared

on their streets. The piano became a symbol of revolution'
(Moussienko, 2016: 12).

This discourse demonstrates the relevance of the approach
used in this academic work to this kind of analysis, which sees the
symbols of Maidan as fundamental factors in the social myth of
Maidan, as essential elements in the manufacturing of collective
imaginaries (Bouchard, 2017) and equally in the social process of
identity formation (Jenkins, 2014). It recognizes too the importance
of the Maidan mythification process (Bouchard, 2017). Only in this
way is it possible to appreciate the power and the impact of the
symbols of Maidan because they do embody the Spirit of Maidan.

3.3.1. The Symbols of Maidan: The Manufacturing of Antagonist Collective Imaginary, and Identity Formation

The concept of antagonist collective imaginary employed in this
work is based on the definition of the collective imaginary
developed by Bouchard (2017): the collective imaginary 'often
refers to all the symbols that a society produces and through which
its members give meaning to their lives. Defined this way, it can
hardly be distinguished from the concept of culture. More
specifically, the collective imaginary includes that which, in the
mental universe, belongs more to the psyche than to reason per se.
And more precisely still, the collective imaginary is characterized
by the link it establishes between familiar realities such as norms,
traditions, narratives, and identities on the one, and, on the other
hand, the deepest symbolic structure. Collective imaginaries
conceived in this way are composed of representations that draw
their authority from the empirical foundation, significant
experiences of a community, and non-rational tools. (…) however,
I would consider it ill-advised to restrict the imaginary to the non-
rational; in the construction of ideologies, the genesis of national
myths, and the formation of discursive strategies, the non-rational
operates but reason nevertheless plays an essential role' (Bouchard,
2017: 13). Bouchard goes on to explain what for him constitute the

four dimensions of the collective imaginary which can be considered the four dimension of antagonist collective imaginary: the unconscious, the cognitive substrates, the analytical categories, and the cultural patterns (Bouchard, 2017: 13-16).

The symbols of Maidan make reference to these dimensions of social imaginary and are essential elements in the production of antagonist collective imaginary.

At the unconscious level, which is the domain of impulses and impetus, instincts, and deep emotions, the symbols of Maidan refer to and carry the experience of a revolution, of awareness, and of wakening. Already during the interviews, I forged the term-category 'zombie Sovieticus' meaning what was left in contemporary Ukrainian of the 'homo Sovieticus'. The 'zombie Sovieticus': is the 'animal identitarium' who has lost its identitarian symbols, rituals, and myths, because these marks and benchmarks of his identity are lost forever, they do not exist anymore; and he is a man without an acknowledgeable identity, a lost relic of the past that still tries to survive nowadays and to retain power. This 'zombie Sovieticus' still lives in the physical and mental dimension of an Ukraine as a 'Waste Land' which 'is a world where people live not out of their own initiative, but out of what they think they're supposed to do, where everybody leading a false life, and where the sense of vitality of life has gone' (Campbell, 1989: 33); and he represents the official collective imaginary and the official habitus.

Maryna Sochenko depicted in her works the features of the 'homo Sovieticus' who decided to rebel and give birth to the Maidan Revolution. Speaking to the author, she said 'the message I want to transmit through my paintings is that these are the real faces of the Maidan revolution. I do agree with your concept of "zombie Sovieticus" because your concept goes straight to the point. Yes, we are like "zombies Sovieticus", we are out of history. We are in transition between wild Russia and civilized Europe, and the message of Maidan was that we are closer to civilized Europe. What is important to understand is that we were part of Russia for more than 300 years. And the message I want to transmit to people is about this war of independence from Russia and Soviet Union.

And I want to show the real face of the real people involved in this revolution, because they are good people not criminals'.

Glib Viches (full name: Glib Vicheslavski; artist, curator, and lecturer in Cultural Studies) encountered the same 'zombie Sovieticus' in search of his/her own cultural space and living space: 'it is real that Maidan transformed people. This Spirit of Maidan (дух) was based on our past and on our idea that every ten years we do a revolution. After the Orange revolution the Ukrainian people were very selfish, they were caring only about themselves and their families. Bur after ten years we started caring about our social life. Festival and gathering were organized and this helped us to understand ourselves more and more'.

The 'zombie Sovieticus' is that individual who continues to live his or her life as if still were in the Soviet system and regime. But in reality, he/she exists as an orphan, feeling a strong sense of loss, incapable of any individual initiative, completely distrustful, suspicious and afraid to be spied upon and controlled everywhere and by everybody like during the totalitarian soviet communist regime. The soul of the 'zombie Sovieticus' is arid, empty, lonely, is turned off; it is the product of a society which lives in constant, disciplined anxiety who has learnt only to whisper. And the 'zombie Sovieticus' represents the official 'habitus', that 'set of dispositions, which incline agents to act and react in certain ways. The dispositions generate practices, perceptions and attitudes which are "regular" without being consciously co-ordinated or governed by any "rule". The dispositions that constitute the habitus are inculcated, structured, durable, generative, and transposable' (Bourdieu, 2005: 12). I presented the newly coined category during the research interviews as well as in the course of an open lecture, which I gave on June 21, 2019 at the Exhibition Center of the Maidan Museum on the topic of 'Art, Identity and Security: the Case of the Maidan Museum'. Both the informants-interviewees and the audience at the lecture responded positively to my 'provocation'; they completely agreed with my concept because they had lived in these very conditions.

The category 'zombie Sovieticus' employed here is what Nobel laureate Svetlana Alexievich (2017: 3) calls the 'sovok': a pejorative term for the Soviet man and woman, struggling to make sense of their past and present in light of the dissolution of the USSR. The sovok lives the sense of loss and humiliation after realizing that the USSR once a great power was now sick and fallen. And he is characterized by apathy and indifference. Therefore, sovok suggests an inert, passive, spiritless person who is completely dependent on the state and is content with whatever he is given, which is not much. For Alexievich 'the "homo Sovieticus" isn't just Russian, he's Belarusian, Turkmen, Ukrainian, Kazakh. Although we now live in separate countries and speak different languages, you couldn't mistake us for anyone else. We're easy to spot! People who've come out of socialism are both like and unlike the rest of humanity — we have our lexicon, our conceptions of good and evil, our heroes, our martyrs. We have a special relationship with death. (...) All of us come from the land of the gulag and harrowing war. Collectivization, dekulakization, mass deportations of various nationalities' (Alexievich, 2017: 4). In her work dedicated to the demise of communism and of the Soviet Union, Alexievich 'sought out people who had been permanently bound to the Soviet idea, letting it penetrate them so deeply that there was no separating them: The state had become their cosmos, blocking out everything else, even their own lives. They couldn't just walk away from History, leaving it all behind and learning to live without it — diving headfirst into the new way of life and dissolving into private existence, like so many others who now allowed what used to be minor details to become their big picture. (…) At heart, we're built for war. We were always either fighting or preparing for war. We've never known anything else — hence our wartime psychology. Even in civilian life, everything was always militarized. The drums were beating, the banners flying, our hearts leaping out of our chests. People didn't recognize their own slavery — they even like being slaves' (Alexievich, 2017: 4).

The 'zombie Sovieticus' is the side effect of a biopolitical experiment like the totalitarian system of the Soviet regime, which in a constant state of exception has reduced the human, the ideal type of 'homo Sovieticus', to bare life, to 'homo sacer', a person who, according to the old Roman law, might not be sacrificed but could be killed with impunity, basically a life utterly without worth. For Agamben (1998) the state relation to homo 'homo sacer' does not cohere around appeals to self-fulfilment or self-actualization but is a relationship of brute force. The 'homo sacer' has none of the civil rights enjoyed by citizens because he/she has not legal, civic, and even political identity.

Thus, the 'zombie Sovieticus' is the 'homo Sovieticus' who, even if they have been liberated from the structural violence of the Soviet Union and lives in another historical period, has not yet acquired a consciousness of himself/herself. They still live like a 'sovok' a 'homo sacer' in a condition of inhibition of action, and still live under a physical and psychological 'structural yoke' and 'post-Soviet condition'. Whilst Galtung (1969) defined structural violence as a form of violence wherein some social structure or social institution may harm people by preventing them from meeting their basic needs, here the category 'structural yoke' means that the still present imagined and practiced Moscow-Soviet yoke prevents the individual from imagining a life other than the one in which he/she lives.

Michael Ignatieff visited Ukraine at the end of the Soviet Empire, and in his book talks about the 'Moscow yoke'. He defines Ukraine as a nuclear superpower (as it briefly was before voluntarily giving up its nuclear weapons), getting its first experience of national independence, and discovering how difficult it is to dig itself out of centuries of Russian rule (Ignatieff, 1994: 10). In his journey through the new independent country, what he noticed was that the people were indeed still oppressed by the Moscow yoke: 'that yoke is still on the Ukrainian people (...) The yoke they wear but do not talk about is the whole weight of the Soviet civilization, and the full weight of it is only to be measured in its totality, in the details: the lift that does not work, the buses held together by bits of wire and string, the windows smeared with dirt everywhere, the casual brutality of all officialdom, the constant humiliation of workers; forcing a woman to earn her living in one hotel I visited by handing out pieces of toilet paper to every man who enters the downstairs hotel toilet. (...) Everyone alive now knew only the Soviet way of life. Behind them lies the only nostalgic paradise of pre-revolutionary peasant Ukraine, the lost world now caricatured in the hotel handicraft shops; beyond their borders lies the impossible world of the capitalist West. Impossible, because it is easy to import video cassettes and blue jeans and condoms and hard currency, but so much more difficult to import Western habits of mind and reconcile them with a Ukranian way of life, to fuse them with a vision of belonging to the here-and-now. There is a devastating innocence in nationalists' faith of independence. Freedom itself is never the end of the road—only the beginning' (Ignatieff, 1994: 106-107).

Borrowing Ignatieff's analogy, Maidan represents significant further steps down that road, but is not in itself the end.

Despite enjoying independence since 1991, and despite the revolutions before the Maidan Revolution, a lot of things went wrong in the democratic and development paths of Ukraine, as reported by Anna Reid (2015) in her recent work 'Borderland—A Journey through the History of Ukraine'. Igor Torbakov (2018) too, in his recent work, identifies the presence of a post-Soviet identity in independent Ukraine which is characterized by political passivity and a reliance on state paternalism, noting the continuance of what he calls a 'post-Soviet condition'. For him, 'the toppling of the Yanukovych regime created an opportunity for a bold political experiment, one largely aimed at accommodating Ukraine's multiple identities and opening up political and economic possibilities to a much broader slice of society. This desire to open up society is what strikes at the very heart of what I call a "post-Soviet condition"—a foundation on which any Putinist political and economic system rests, along with extensive corruption. In the broad historical view, the disintegration of the Soviet Union was always bound to be a protracted process. True, the Soviet Union as a state (or, in a memorable phase, "as a geopolitical reality") did indeed disappear overnight. But the decomposition of Soviet institutions, practices, and the political mindset have taken decades, and the process is still going on. Among the characteristic features of the post-Soviet condition are the huge spill-over of the old (Soviet) elites; a state in which power is wielded by a narrow, tightknit group of people who cannot be easily be removed from power; and a system in which the rule of law does not exist, the legislature is a rubber-stamp, and there is no genuine space for political and economic competition. Ukraine's post-independence experience has a somewhat typical post-Soviet trajectory. Upon gaining independence in 1991, Ukraine was effectively an empty shell, not a full-blown nation-state (or rather state-nation) with its distinct identity. This shell was eventually filled largely with post-Soviet content: authoritarian political practices, crony capitalism, and the merger of politics and big business that stifled competition' (Torbakov, 2018: 195-196).

Despite generational change, in Ukraine the 'zombie Sovieticus' 'sovok', and 'homo sacer' mentality survive, a mentality of apathy and indifference. As was demonstrated by the various interviews recorded here, and despite the best efforts of these many artists and activists, Ukrainian society is still an inhibited one which whispers rather than speaks openly.

The second dimension of the antagonist collective imaginaries is constituted by the cognitive substrates, the deep mental structures, the great cross-cultural matrices, often ahistorical, or pre-existing from earlier times, which are present in the symbols of Maidan. These include fire, Taras Shevchenko (national poet of Ukraine), Cossack 'Mamai' with 'bandura' (the hero who goes around the world and helps people), Cossack's hair style (khokhol-oseledets), Ukrainian Cossack camp (named 'sich' [укр. Сiч]) which existed from the 16th to the 18th century (during the Revolution of Dignity the camp on Independence Square was called 'Maidanna Sich'), and Malevich's 'Black square'. These symbols are archetypes which constitute key elements of the DNA of Ukrainian identity. Bouchard defines archetypes as 'stable forms, observable in most cultures at various periods—for example, initial chaos, the search for origins, creation and the end of the world, the appeal and fear of the supernatural, the insoluble bonds of blood, the eternal return, the new-born saviour, metamorphosis, renewal or rebirth, return to the place of origin, original sin, the Apocalypse (and itsmany secular variantssuch as climate or nuclear catastrophes), treason, revenge, martyrdom or sacrifice of the expiatory victim, exodus, and so on' (Bouchard, 2017: 14).

Neda Nedjana in her play 'Maidan Inferno' uses the concept and the image of fire as an element, which protects the protestors from the attack of the 'riot police-force of evil'. The words and images of the national poet and spiritual founder of Ukraine Taras Shevchenko are reproduced in various objects preserved in the Maidan Museum. One example is his wooden statue (figure 34) which was in Maidan during the Revolution of Dignity.

Figure 34. Wooden statue of Taras Shevchenko. (Photo credit: G. Ercolani, 2019)

Taras Shevchenko's manipulated image is still present in the area of 'the Maidan', as a mural; it says: 'The fire won't burn the seasoned', and is a work of the street artist Sociopath, the Ukrainian Bansky (figure 35).

Figure 35. Mural representing Taras Shevchenko. (Photo credit: G. Ercolani, 2019).

The three 'Cossack' archetypes Cossack 'mamai' with 'bandura' (the hero who goes around the world and helps people; figure 36), Cossack's hair style (khokhol-oseledets), and a Ukrainian Cossack camp in the 17th century (Euromaidan square) represented the major identitarian reference in the Maidan. As Reid (2015) and Plokhy (2012; 2015) have demonstrated in their works, the romantic image and the myth of the Cossack are central in the construction of the Ukrainian national identity. The reproduction of Cossack traditions was visible in the organization of the Maidan, which was organized as a Cossack camp, in the organization of the protestors in 'hundreds', like Cossack military units, in the image of male protestors who cut their hair in the typical Cossack style, and in the presence of Cossack music groups.

Figure 36. Kozak Mamai, folk painting. Late 19th-early 20th century, courtesy of the Maidan Museum

And Ivan Semesyuk, using an apparently child-like, iconoclast approach, gives his own interpretation of the Cossack tradition in his work 'The Cossack Cat' (figure 37). Here the cat parades its Cossack air style and is wearing a jump suit which everyone is now wearing in Ukraine.

The whole of Semesyuk's Maidan works of art are characterized by an iconoclast style and humour as an epistemological tool and epistemic practice.

Figure 37. The 'Kozak Cat' by Ivan Semesyuk, courtesy of the Maidan Museum

However, Ivan Semesyuk's art makes reference to another controversial Ukrainian myth-hero: Stepan Bandera, whose images appeared in Maidan (figure 38).

Ivan: 'this is a handmade embroidery work, and the topic is Stepan Bandera. And it says "you were Jew, but you were anti-Semite". This work was made because the Russian media were saying that Ukraine is an anti-Semitic country and that we are against Jews. We want to show to the world that we are not as we are portrayed by the Russian media. Our president and our prime minister are Jews, therefore, this is very original for a Bandera's country'.

Figure 38. Embroidery work by Ivan Semesyuk. (Photo credit: G. Ercolani, 2019)

Malevich's 'Black square' is in the category of archetypes too, and Sophie Pinkham explains why: 'in 1915, a century before Maidan, Kazimir Malevich painted a black square on a white background. When it was first exhibited, the painting hung in the upper corner of the room, the place traditionally reserved, in Russian homes, for a religious icon. The black Square became the icon of the Russian avant-garde, hanging above Malevich's body when he lay in state in his Leningrad apartment in 1935. (...) Malevich was born to Polish parents near Kiev; his work was influenced both by the black and red patterns of traditional Ukrainian textiles and by the black crosses on the garments of Russian saints. Today, like many heroes from the Soviet Union and the Russian Empire, he is claimed by Russian, Poles, and Ukrainians alike. For Malevich, the Black Square represented the end of time, the culmination of history. (...) For him, truth began at zero. (...) His black Square was meant to evoke "experience of pure non-objectivity in the white emptiness of a liberal nothing." By the time the Russian Revolution and ensuing civil war were over, in 1922, this "emptiness of liberated nothing" was painfully real, with everyday life shattered by the conflict between the Red Army and the anti-communist White Guards. Over the next decades, the Soviets built a new world, with millions of causalities along the way. But by 1991 the countries of the former Soviet Union found themselves at another zero point, forced to reinvent and rebuild yet again. And then there was Maidan. More than a hundred people were killed during the protest; some ten thousand died in the war that followed. Ukraine and Russia, which supported and prolonged the conflict, descended into paranoia and rage' (Pinkham, 2016: xii-xiii).

It was Glib Viches who brought Malevich's Black Square to the Maidan events and discourse. He brought it to the 'holy corner', like Malevich who hung the Black Square in the 'holy corner' of his room, which in Russian homes was reserved for religious icons. Glib, like the other artists who were interviewed, participated to the Maidan. His artistic discourse is based on performance – his presence, carrying a flag reproducing Malevich's Black Square in Maidan Square (figure 39) and on the Lenin's pedestal (figure 40) – which can be interpreted as a kind of intervention-appropriation of the space, as can, indeed, the collages he made with objects left in Maidan square, objects that he saw as having a unique aura. In Ukraine, Malevich's Black Square was well known and the purpose of Glib's performance art in the Maidan Square and on the Lenin pedestal was equally well understood to mean the re-creation of Ukraine in Maidan itself. Through the very visibility of his art, Glib pushed people to look at modern Ukrainian art, which therefore had impact and which likewise appropriated both space and discourse. For Glib, Malevich is important because 'Malevich was looking for objects-symbols which were Ukrainian country life. In the old Ukrainian houses there was a stove, which warmed the house, and this stove was painted before important holidays. At the same time there was a trunk in which people kept their things. According to Malevich both were the symbols of Ukrainian rural life and he travelled around Ukraine searching for symbols of countryside people's lives. Thes geometric shapes made by Malevich refer to this precise Ukrainian symbolism'. Definitely in Glib Viches' definition of Malevich's art it is possible to appreciate the Black Square as an important archetype in the construction of the Ukrainian identity. At the same time, it echoes the European modernism emerging in the west at the same time. And through his performance and in carrying the Black Square, he converted the Maidan Square in the 'holy corner' of new Ukraine.

Figure 39. Malevich's Black Square in Maidan, courtesy of Glib Viches.

Glib, however, in his performances, was carrying another flag too representing the Vasarely's Zebra, an element communicating another message present in his artistic discourse. His performance on Lenin's pedestal (figure 36) speaks for itself as an act to desacralize a holy, untouchable myth of the past regime, but still present in the space of Kyiv. Because Maidan was at the same time 'a symbolic farewell to the Soviet past—the demolition of remaining monuments to Lenin, more than five hundred altogether, in a few weeks—and the Revolution of Dignity' (Plokhy, 2015: 352).

Figure 40. Viches' works and performance on Lenin pedestal, courtesy of Glib Viches.

In the words of Glib: 'people were very happy about what I was doing in Maidan, and in Ukraine everybody knows about the Malevich Black Square, it is about our cultural heritage. And about the zebra people know about Vasarely (1938) too. I wanted to present two symbols and put them together: Malevich's Black Square which represents Ukrainian art, and Vasarely's Zebra which I consider to be the symbol of Western art. (...) Mine are historical art symbols and people in Maidan understood them. Because what happened in Maidan was "modern"; in Maidan "Modern Ukraine" was present. And in Maidan, I collected material, which was left behind: pieces of burn tyres, pieces of Molotov bottles, gas masks, gloves, etc, and with them I produced collages. I was collecting these materials because I was worrying that after the Revolution all these objects were going to be lost, dispersed, and forgotten'.

Moreover, non-visual elements must be added to the symbols of Maidan. This forms a distinctive dimension which is part of the collective imaginaries in the cognitive substrates: music. The music played by Taras Kompanichenko and Valery Hladunets belongs to the Ukrainian identity archetypes.

Figure 41. Taras Kompanichenko. (Photo credit: G. Ercolani, 2019)

Taras Kompanichenko (figure 41), known worldwide for his Ukrainian music, participated in the Maidan, and before that he took part in the Orange Revolution (2004-2005). He plays, among other musical instruments, the 'kobza', the lute used by the Ukrainian minstrels known as 'kobzari, on which he plays very old songs, some dating back to the seventeenth century. His musical production is an embodiment of the Ukrainian national idea, the romantic fantasy of Cossack heroes and pastoral patriots. Taras' image provided by Sophie Pinkham is similar to the one I had when I met him at the 'Information and Exhibition Center of the Maidan Museum' for our interview in which Taras played and explained to me the meanings and the origins of his music: 'he was dressed in full Cossack regalia: loose "sharovary" pants suitable for riding on horseback, long, pointy shoes and a tie woven in a traditional Ukrainian pattern. His hair was closely shaved except for the Cossack "oseledets", or "herring", a long, graying plume on the top of his head. For convenience, he had wound his forelock around his ear. His thick, dark brown mustache curled up at the ends. This was not a protest costume, or a means of attracting tourists; this was how he got dressed for work' (Pinkham, 2016: 214-215). This is how Taras recalls his moments in the Maidan and how he became an activist serving the Maidan community: 'first I came to Maidan to protest against the president of Ukraine for not signing the agreement with EU. I was one of the people that wanted to show our values, and principles. However, I remember, I was playing in a place close to Maidan, it was the day for the commemoration of the Holomodor genocide of the Ukrainian people (famine). Someone, who was present at my concert invited me to play and sing at Maidan. Then, the following day, I started singing at Maidan, and I started singing Holodomor songs. While I was singing, someone from the audience shouted to me to sing about freedom. In my repertoire, there is a song "De Libertate" and I started singing this song, which is basically how I started to sing and play in Maidan. When Maidan started, I was in Maidan, and people asked me to play different songs. At that time Maidan was not crowded, but when Maidan started to be the center of the demonstrations and more people started to gather there, I started to sing different songs. These songs were not written by me, like the case of "De Libertate", but they were popular songs, and people joined me like a chorus. And I was singing songs of the Ukrainian Independence War (1917-1921). After that moment I started to go to Maidan everynight and sing songs with the people. There was nothing political in Maidan during night time. At midnight a priest was coming to the stage, we were praying together, then I was reading the news, and then I started to play my instrument. I use to sing Ukrainian songs, choral, religious songs. Special choral songs dedicated to the Virgin Mary and songs of the Independence War (1917-1921). I got pneumonia there. It was pure happiness. It was a great responsibility, and it was an honour to me to be there serving during the night shift of the 18-19 Feb 2014 (during the big fight). I remember I was singing on the Maidan stage and the police snipers were pointing their laser to my mouth'.

Taras has investigated the heritage of earlier music too, and has collected and preserved for the future thousands and thousands of old Ukrainian songs. However, as Pinkham has noticed, in Taras' embodiment of the Cossack myth 'it was fitting that he shared his first name with Taras Shevchenko, the poet-prophet of the Ukrainian nation who wrote a book called "Kobzar" (minstrel) and was often called a "kobzar" himself, though he was not a musician. In the nineteenth century, Taras Shevchenko had wept over Cossack burial mounds, writing poems that glorified a mythical Ukrainian past; now Taras Kompanichenko was carrying on this tradition' (Pinkham, 2016: 215-216).

Valery Hladunets (figure 42) joined and supported Maidan from the beginning. He came to Maidan with his music group to play traditional Ukrainian folk songs, and his experience is illuminating: 'I was singing folk-classical songs from all Ukraine. I am a music anthropologist. I have recorded traditional folk songs from all around Ukraine and after that I reproduced them. Maidan was not only a revolution for dignity but a Cultural Revolution too. Ukrainian people had the possibility of rediscovering Ukrainian culture in order to help the Ukrainian identity blossom. All this Ukrainian culture was forbidden during the Soviet time. Taras Kompanichenko, the musician you met, did a great job in rediscovering in Ukrainian archives very old traditional Ukrainian music, songs, and poems. All these represent the Ukrainian cultural heritage'.

Figure 42. Valery Hladunets. (Photo credit: G. Ercolani, 2019)

It must be added that as an anthropologist of folk music Valery conducted research around Ukraine. And his experience as researcher is interesting because it unfolds the reality around the Ukrainian folk music, which was little known by the general audience or, indeed, in academic circles. As Valery explains: 'in the past scholars searched for these traditions of Ukrainian culture but they were interested in producing a Soviet discourse, not a Ukrainian one. The Soviet discourse was falsifying the Ukrainian cultural heritage, because the aim of the discourse was the fabrication of the Soviet man. Another reason for not having this research performed before was financial. Academic institutions simply do not have financial resources for such musicological research. At that time (1999) I did not receive any financial aid from my university for my research. And I think I started searching for old Ukrainian folk music because of my childhood. I remember my grandmother preparing the bread and while baking it was singing Ukrainian songs. It was a kind of ritual, of magic. And I was listening to these songs and music.' Valery and his group played traditional National Religious Music, traditional music, and patriotic music (the Ukrainian national anthem and Ukrainian hymns). However, as Valery said, Taras has investigated more than twenty Ukrainian hymns, and more than 300.000 Ukrainian traditional songs'.

The third dimension of antagonistic collective imaginaries, which is close to the last one (the cognitive substrates) includes 'very common analytical categories that support thought, such as change-stability, break-continuity, identity-otherness, sacred-secular, centre-periphery, inclusion-exclusion polarities, and also perceptions of space, concepts of time seen as linear or cyclical, constellations of events, and so on' (Bouchard, 2017: 14). The following Maidan symbols fit into this analytical category: Yolka (Christmas tree), tyres (burned tyres) helmets (reinterpreted painted helmets), shields (reinterpreted painted shields), fire barrels, Molotov cocktails, Tryzub (the trident –on the state coat of arms of Ukraine), and the blue-yellow colours that are the national colours of Ukraine. And this is for the simple reason that these symbols acquired a new meaning through the Maidan events and really represent the 'tools', with which the analytical categories of in-out, we-the other, etc., were fabricated.

The 'Yolka' represented a Christmas tree for the people of Maidan, as Sasha Komyakhov explained to me: 'Yolka is the Christmas tree of Maidan, it is *the* Christmas tree of Maidan revolution. People coming from different parts of Ukraine to join the Maidan Revolution brought their flags that were attached to the Yolka. The tradition of the Christmas tree in the Maidan Square already existed before the revolution. The name of this tree in Ukrainian is "yalinka", but after the mistake of the Ukrainian President Viktor Fedorovich Yanukovich, who called the "yalinka" "yolka" everybody started to call this very specific Christmas tree "yolka" and it became one of the symbols of Maidan. The installation of yalinka-yolka in Maidan Square before Christmas was the main pretext used by the government to push the protesters out of Maidan. Now when somebody talks about yolka the reference is to this tree of the Maidan revolution'.

The burned tyres have a particular significance in dividing the field of struggle into two opposing camps, pro-Maidan vs. against-

Maidan. The painted helmets and the painted shields were used by the protestors to defend themselves from the attack of the 'against-Maidan' forces. Yulia Ovcharenko reminisced that 'in my mind I have a very clear symbol of Maidan which is the fire barrel. It represents all the people united, it represents union. The people were gathering together around the fire barrel to warm themselves, and at the same time fire is magic. Fire is a symbol which carries the idea of life and death'.

For Yuriy Gruzinov, the symbols of Maidan were the tear gas bomb (used by the police) and the Molotov cocktail: 'the police were throwing us tear gas bombs and we were responding with Molotov bombs. The Molotov bomb is like a language. Symbols must have power inside and the cocktail Molotov is the most powerful symbol, it can explode like the society can explode. The Molotov bomb represents the explosive side of society. The Molotov is the explosive reaction of the angry people of Ukraine'.

The 'Tryzub' (the trident from the state coat of arms of Ukraine) is for Ivan Semesyuk 'a stamp that legitimized all our actions in Maidan. At the same time, it is an anti-Soviet symbol, therefore, it is a symbol above all other symbols'.

Finally, blue and yellow are the colours of the Ukrainian National Flag, and as Sasha Komyakhov suggested, 'even if the Police were using the same flag, in Maidan the meaning was different. We shared the same flag but with different meaning. Everybody who came to Maidan and left Maidan were wearing yellow-blue ribbons. These ribbons became the insignia of the people of Maidan and of the people who supported Maidan'.

Cultural patterns are the fourth component of the antagonist collective imaginaries. Cultural patterns are defined by Bouchard as 'socially produced collective representations and therefore more linked to the contexts. I am thinking of visions of the self and others, of the past and the future, as well as ideals and norms that set collective goals and guide behaviours. (...) Cultural patterns also includes ideological constructs conceives to overcome the contradictions that every society faces at various moments in its history' (Bouchard, 2017: 14-15). It is this component which helps us perceive the 'symbols of Maidan' as 'symbols of community', where the very community becomes a symbol too. The 'symbols of Maidan', all of them, are to be considered as signs of identity, and they refer to the construction of the new-Ukrainian identity, which is based on the strong intention to move toward European values and to distance itself from Russia, Russian influence and Russian cultural domination. For Richard Jenkins 'identity is the human capacity — rooted in language — to know "who's who" (and hence "what's what"). This involves knowing who we are, us knowing who they think we are and so on. This is a multi-dimensional classification or mapping of the human world and our places in it, as individuals and as members of collectivities. (...) It is a process — identification — not a "thing"; it is not something that one can have, or not, it is something that one does. (...) Identification has to made to matter, through the power of symbols and ritual experiences, for example' (Jenkins, 2014: 6-7).

All the symbols of Maidan came from the protest, a protest made in the name of identity and dignity. And Sasha Komyakhov considers the very protest itself a symbol too, a symbol which divides between two fields, the Ukrainian and the Russian: 'another symbol is represented by the concept of protest, to protest. For example, for Russian people it was difficult to understand how so many people had such common ideas (or were united in one common idea?) and how they all gathered together to protest. For people from former Soviet countries the very idea of protest is difficult if not inconceivable. Therefore, the Russian propaganda tried to explain that people were protesting because in their food and drink something special was mixed, perhaps a poison, and people were intoxicated. The Russian propaganda media were broadcasting the narrative that people were protesting because of some drug present in their food and drinks. However, in Maidan there was no alcohol, people were drinking basically tea'. In reality, the Russian authorities were acting like the ones described in 'Myth and Madness', the novel of Hryhorczuk (2016: 20-21), where, using a former Soviet punitive medicine approach, they defined the Maidan events as a 'philosophical intoxication' and Euromaidan as madness and an infectious disease.

Ivan Semesyuk points his finger to the relationship between concepts of identity and post-colonial discourse: 'before Maidan we were living in a post-colonial discourse. During Maidan we wanted, as now, to delete the colonial term, the very word "colonial". We are in a post-post-colonial time. At the same time there was not a precise ideology in Maidan. Our ideology was Ukrainianeness, we wanted to be ourselves, to speak and write in our Ukrainian language. Our identity is in our language. Our Ukrainian language and culture were so much oppressed in the old time. Now we want to produce culture in our own language. In modern Ukraine we have less and less people producing culture, and writing in Russian. On the other hand, it is a great pity that some great culture was produced in Russian but went nowhere. In the new, future Ukraine, less people will speak, write, and understand Russian. Therefore, this cultural struggle is a question of survival. The same happened in Czechoslovakia with the German language, and in Croatia with Serbian. Basically, we are pursuing the same process'.

The same tone is assumed by Taras Kompanichenko, for whom his awakening goes hand in hand with the empowerment of Ukrainian culture: 'I was a political dissident who had been supporting democracy in Ukraine. Back to the year 1988, I participated to all the political demonstrations for example the one on Chernobyl disaster, against the forced camp. I was caught by the police. I was persecuted by the police during the regime. Already back to 1988 we were fighting for the Ukrainian language and culture. We tried to preserve the main Ukrainian building (elements of our own identity), like the religious buildings. During the Soviet time lot of Ukrainian buildings and monuments were destroyed. The same happened to our Ukrainian culture. Our case was different from other Soviet countries. Poland was invaded by USSR, but they continued to speak their own language and no one was calling them nationalists. All the original Ukrainian institutions were destroyed by Russia and the Soviet Union: The Ukrainian church, the Ukrainian nobility, the Ukrainian language, our classic literature. During the Soviet time, our national classic literature was forbidden. However, the same did not happen in other Warsaw Pact countries (East Germany, Poland, Romania, Bulgaria and so on). The USSR destroyed Ukrainian dignity. To Ukraine was given only a visible frame of identity, meaning: "you have your culture, but you cannot use it too much". But now we are ready to claim back our culture and to be a modern country. The USSR was always humiliating Ukraine. We are depicted as nationalist, but after the implosion of the USSR we want to bring back our national culture and language. For us to be a nationalist is not a bad thing; it is to recuperate our culture. The Maidan revolution is one of our revolutions, however, I do not like revolution. They bring chaos and economic problems. The Maidan revolution was about a democratic Ukraine and for our European aspirations. Revolution is the gap for the Ukraine to fight for democracy and human rights. Moscow propaganda depicts the Ukrainian project as an USA project, but this is not the case. Moscow propaganda is manipulating the perception of the Ukrainian revolution'.

These cultural patterns are thus converted into an ideology, a more organised system of thinking, and in the specific project of politics a project of belonging, 'that is, it is a project that is based on belonging to one (or more) group(s) and not to others. Group membership depends on an identification with the group: such identification might be made on the basis of gender, religion, sexual practice, nationality, race, or one of a number of other identificatory categories. (...) Such identificatory practices are central to all forms of identity-formation and also involve dis-identification from other categories. Identity has to be considered relationally, and so, too, does identity politics' (Lawler, 2018: 163).

However, there is an image donated to this research by Sasha Komyakhov and which summarizes the full human tragedy of collective imaginaries. As Komyakhov noted: 'as for an academic work, I think this picture (figure 43) would fit. This is an allegorical illustration, in which an old sick countrywoman sits home in the far village worrying for her son who has gone away to join the revolution. She can't go there herself and can only imagine the lights of Maidan in her window. In a way it represents Ukrainians:

we can share rightful and global values but most of us see them as some kind of mirage'.

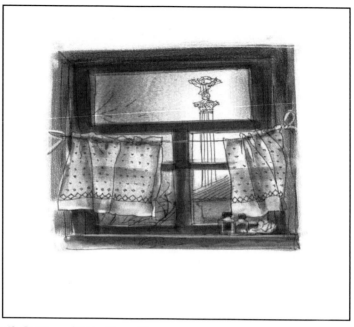

Figure 43. Courtesy of Sasha Komyakhov

The contribution of the symbols of Maidan is essential to the antagonist collective imaginaries of post-Maidan Ukraine. However, based on Bouchard (2017: 16-18), these antagonist collective imaginaries establish and perpetuate eight types of representations that together form the basis for the constitutive relationships of a culture. And, as has been argued, the symbols of Maidan do play a fundamental role in these representations: representations of space, representations of time, representations of the social, representations of the self and others, representations of the past, representations of the future, representations of the nation or society, and representations of the universe, life and death, this world and the hereafter. This demonstrates the strong connection between artistic production, identity formation, and politics, and shows the importance of Maidan in order to reimagine and redefine the Ukrainian identities.

3.4.   Conclusion

This chapter has unwrapped the concepts around the definition of Maidan as a 'social myth' (Bouchard, 2017). Therefore, using both the theory and the results of the fieldwork, it has provided illustrations, in the specific context of Maidan, of the concepts of social myth (Bouchard, 2017), of myth-metalanguage (Barthes, 2000), of spiritual place (Hryhorczuk, 2016), of anthropological place (Augé, 2011), of emotional field (Beatty, 2019), and of chosen trauma (Volkan, 1999, 2004, 2006; Svasek, 2005). Then, focusing on the relevance of the art of Maidan and the interviews with its practitioners, the chapter presents the role of art in the Maidan events, and has identified the symbols of Maidan. The art of Maidan, carries an aura, a tension, an imminence. It has been considered 'conceptual art' which is an essential element (1) in the manufacturing of antagonist collective imaginaries (Bouchard, 2017); (2) in the Maidan mythification process (Bouchard, 2017); (3) in the social process of identity formation (Jenkins, 2014); and (4) shows the strong relation between identity-identification-interpellation (Althusser, 1988; Ranciere, 2014).

4
The Spirit of Maidan and
the Maidanization Process

4.1. Introduction

This chapter summarizes the main traits and properties of the Spirit of Maidan and unravels the character of the Maidanization process.

4.2. The Spirit of Maidan

The Spirit of Maidan is like the breath of God which gave life to Adam, and which transforms the 'zombie Sovieticus' into the 'homo Maidan'- that at any rate is the claim, the cry of the new 'homo Maidan' which replaces the whisper of the 'Homo Sovieticus'. It is the wake of imagination free from the imposition of an inhibited society.

The essence of the Spirit of Maidan is fabricated as a struggle for personal and civil freedoms against injustice, human right and dignity, governmental corruption, tyranny, despotism, in the pursuit of European values. It is a pursuit of cultural independence in which the Ukrainian language is the language of the 'homo Maidan'. It is the site of a rediscovery, and revaluation of the Ukrainian culture which years of Soviet yoke had denigrated, humiliated, and cancelled. It is, or is intended to be, a new and different way to imagine the Ukraine of the future. And this European orientation looks not just to a political but also to a "civilizational" choice. 'Those in Ukraine who opt for "Europe" simply want to put an end to ugly post-Soviet practices (such as rapacious crony capitalism, corruption, nepotism, selective application of justice, etc.) and foster the rule of law, secure property rights, and protection of human dignity — the values they associate, correctly, with Europe' (Torbakov, 2018: 196).

Taras Kompanichenko made very clear this point of the European orientation: 'it is very interesting: we were going toward Europe but we discovered Ukraine. The mix between European values and our Ukrainian culture were the ingredients of our struggle against Russia. The Maidan event was a shock for the political class too, because the people became conscious. The Maidan consciousness'. That the idea of Europe this notion imagines is itself in some respects mythic and in important respects at best an over-simplification is not relevant to its importance in the dialogue in Maidan. On the one hand it represents a potent rejection of the Soviet past and Russian present, and on the other hand it embodies an aspiration which Ukrainians involved in Maidan or animated by the Spirit of Maidan share.

Therefore, the Spirit of Maidan represents that future which becomes a new cultural fact based on imagination, anticipation, and aspiration. And imagination 'is a vital resource in all the social processes and projects, and needs to be seen as a quotidian energy, not visible only in dreams, fantasies, and sequestered moments of euphoria and creativity' (Appadurai, 2013: 287). The Spirit of Maidan has triggered and animated a politics of possibility, in which the Ukrainian society strongly wants to organize the future as a cultural horizon in which the capacity to aspire is one of its revolutionary hallmarks. The capacity to aspire, which for Appadurai, is 'conceived as a cultural capacity, especially among the poor, the future-oriented logic of development could find a natural ally, and the poor could find the resources required to contest and alter the conditions of their own poverty' (Appadurai, 2013: 179).

4.3.   The 'Maidanization Process'

One result of this fieldwork research is the fact that it is now possible to see 'the Maidan' (social myth), the symbols of Maidan, and the Maidan Museum and its activities as a whole system. And these three elements are united by a common praxis that may be called 'the Maidanization process'. That praxis of the Maidanization process is translated in 'doing', i.e. being present in Maidan, and in its perpetuation. For this reason, the 'Maidanization process' is seen as the combination of the Maidan mythification process (Bouchard, 2017) with the Maidan societal securitization ritual (Ercolani, 2016). This step is based on Bouchard according to whom the 'ritual takes its meaning from myth. In return, it helps strengthen and renew it' (Bouchard, 2017: 39). Therefore, myth and its ritual and symbol, must been considered as a whole, which here is called the 'Maidanization process'. It is through the 'Maidanization process' that humankind as an 'animal identitarium' creates his myths, symbols, and rituals which represent his own identity. And based on the results of my fieldwork experience I can affirm that the 'Maidanization process' was lived as an enormous and contaminating ritual which 'is the enactment of a myth: by participating in the rite, you participate in the myth. Myths don't count if they're just hitting your rational faculties — they have to hit the heart. You have to absorb them and adjust to them to make them your life. And insofar as the myth is a revelation of dimensions of your own spiritual potential, you are activating those dimensions in yourself and experiencing them' (Campbell, 1989: 35).

The 'Maidanization process' produced socio-cultural and symbolic capital (Bourdieu, 2005), embodied by the 'Spirit of Maidan' (дух); and participated in the production of the aura of the art of Maidan. The 'Spirit of Maidan' gave the breath of life to the 'homo Maidan' who represents a paradigm (Kuhn, 1996: x) and a 'habitus' (Bourdieu, 2005), which participate not in a scientific, but a socio-cultural revolution inside the field (Bourdieu, 2005) of the Ukrainian identity, in which the new paradigm-habitus ('homo Maidan') fights to replace the old paradigm-habitus ('zombie Sovieticus').

The Maidanization process becomes the symbolic-cultural-identitarian paradigm of reference of the post-Maidan 'animal identitarium', in which the nature of mankind as 'animal symbolicum' (Cassirer, 1972), as producer and consumer of myth, and as 'homo ritualis' (Lisón Tolosana, 2012), the human being who experiences his life through rituals, is transformed into that of the 'homo Maidan'.

In short, as discussed in the previous chapter, the 'Maidanization process' assembled an antagonist socio-cultural paradigm-habitus of reference for the construction of the post-

Maidan Ukrainian identity, in which the art and the symbols of Maidan do play an important role. In the following, the research will first analyse the Maidan mythification process and then the Maidan societal securitization process.

As noted above 'social myths borrow from archetypes and other images conveyed by allegorical, religious, and philosophical myths—from literature (the epic and the heroic aspects), religion (divine origins, the concept of the Chosen People invested with a divine mission), or philosophy (visions of the world, teleology)' (Bouchard, 2017: 31).

However, for Bouchard 'social myths are usually the product of a mythification process—not to be confused with mystification—that involves no fewer than eight elements that contribute to shaping a powerful message' (Bouchard, 2017: 48). And these elements are: (1) The Construction of the Subject; (2) Anchors; (3) Imprints; (4) Ethos; (5) Sacralization; (6) The Narrative; (7) Techniques of Persuasion: and (8) Social Actors (Bouchard, 2017: 48-92). Each of these can be considered in turn.

The construction of the subject: 'mythification presupposes first of all the construction or identification of a subject: Who are we talking about? Who is the mythical discourse intended for?' (Bouchard, 2017: 48). Maidan as a social myth talks to the Ukrainian people, it wants to emancipate the country from the colonial power of Russia, it fights for a Ukrainian identity based on European values and a recognition of the Ukrainian language and culture. This means that Ukraine, through the Maidan events, has initiated a process of deep identity renewal, which has implied a symbolic redefinition.

The anchors: the concept of anchors 'refers to an event or to a sequence of structuring events occurring in the recent or distant past that play a role of anchors. This is the meaning that is usually given to the concept of founding myth. (...) Anchors can be based on events that are both traumatic and achievements' (Bouchard, 2017: 49). The Maidan is the event that constitutes the founding myth, the anchor to Maidan social myth. As has been demonstrated, the Maidan was a traumatic event and represents a political achievement for the results that it brought. A characteristic of the anchors is that they wait to be awakened, and this is basically what happened, and the people of Maidan were, indeed, awakened. And this is the mission of the Maidan Museum too, to preserve the Spirit of Maidan, and to awake the Ukrainian people.

Imprints: 'experience that is raised to the rank of anchor leaves in the collective consciousness an imprint that takes the form of a profound, lasting emotion. In the case of a negative anchor, the emotion is very often fuelled by a wound and is expressed as suffering and mourning' (Bouchard, 2017: 52). The killing of the Heavenly Hundred has contributed to convert the Maidan into a memorial space visited by people who want to remember and commemorate the heroes of the Revolution of Dignity. That imprint finds a material form in many of the objects in the museum and a spiritual form in its enduring emotional memories.

Ethos: 'the fourth element of the mythification process consists in the translation of the imprint into the ethos, understood as a set of aspirations, beliefs, principles, values, ideals, moral standards, vision of the world, and attitudes, or deep predispositions. For example, it is possible for a strong sense of injustice (imprint) linked to some experience of colonization or domination (anchor) to generate a quest for equality, equity, and democracy. An episode of collective humiliation is likely to generate a valorization of pride, a constant quest for respect' (Bouchard, 2017: 53). And Maidan was the sincere reaction of humiliated people, tired of remaining under the indirect control of Russia, and eager to create a new identity and future.

Sacralization: for Bouchard 'sacralization is the crucial stage in the formation of the social myth. It lies at the heart of what could be called its immune system; it is above all thanks to this attribute that myth can endure and survive opposition and contradictions' (Bouchard, 2017: 57). To the sacralisation is associated the cognitive shift meaning that 'emotion takes over from reason as the primary engine of consciousness. Through this transformation, which opens the way to sacredness, social myths transcend other collective representations, in particular the symbolic "resources" that make up "repertoires" (symbols, customs, traditions, model of behaviour, etc.)' (Bouchard, 2017: 57). What made possible this cognitive shift in the case of the social Myth of Maidan was some form of transcendence, of 'catharsis', which was expressed by the participants in the Maidan, to push beyond the limitations of daily life, the need to fight for dignity and recognition. The sacralisation is present in the aura carried by the whole of the art of Maidan.

The narrative: 'this component consists primarily in the construction of a narrative supported by practices of commemoration. The goal of this is to activate the emotion associated with the anchor and the imprint in order to bolster the ethos. Ritual plays a key role here. It translates abstract values into actual experiences, reinforced by dramatizations intended to create or intensify the sense of belonging. It also establishes or evokes symbols that embody these values, giving them concrete features; such symbols include notable sites, objects, or figures and triumphant or sacrificed heroes. (...) Finally, the narrative itself — or, more broadly, the construction of memory — uses various channels: iconography, historical scholarship, stories and legends, museum, the novel, the media, and historical re-enactments' (Bouchard, 2017: 59). Maidan has produced narratives and now the main commemorations are kept alive by the Maidan Museum. Moreover, the Maidan Museum publishes academic papers focused on the Maidan itself. These narratives differ in some ways; each person has their own perspective. But at the same time, they draw together to form a common set of threads which sustain and promote the symbols explained in the previous chapter and the experiences they present.

Techniques of persuasion: 'obeying the same logic as narrative, techniques of persuasion are aimed at formulating or reformulating the central message of the myth according to changing challenges, publics, and contexts' (Bouchard, 2017: 64). One area of the techniques of persuasion, in which the art of Maidan has been particularly active, and which the Maidan Museum now continues, is that of repertoires of discursive patterns. Maidan has provided for the creation of the post-Maidan Ukrainian identity those national repertoires or 'symbolic patterns to which the members of a disadvantaged and marginalized class or group can refer in order to define and valorize their identity, restore a sense of dignity, as well as their place in society' (Bouchard, 2017: 75).

Social actors: 'The final element in the mythification process consists in the work of familiar social actors such as government, political parties, unions, the education system, churches, activists, social classes, and the media. (...) The fate of social myth is a matter of power relations' (Bouchard, 2017: 80). Here the social actor is represented by the Maidan Museum, and next chapter will analyse the problems of the museum with power-structures deeply unhappy both with its very establishment and with its activities.

Having presented the Maidan mythification process, it is now the moment to introduce the next element in the fabrication of the 'Maidanization process', the Maidan societal securitization process. To explain this, the argument touches briefly on current notions of securitization in the 'critical security studies' literature.

The image of the Maidan societal securitization ritual is attached to the concept of societal security itself. The societal arena is one of the security sectors (military, political, economic, societal, and environmental) developed by Buzan, Waever and de Wilde (1998) in their analysis of the multiple faces of security. It refers explicitly to the concept of identity: 'the organizing concept in the societal sector is identity. Societal insecurity exists when communities of whatever kind define a development or potentiality as a threat to their survival as community. (...) Societal security is about large, self-sustaining identity groups. (...) The concept could also be understood as "identity security". (...) Societal security is about collectives and their identity. (...) The concept of societal security, however, refers to the level of collective identities and action taken to defend such "we identities"' (Buzan, Waever and de Wilde, 1998: 119-120).

However, the Maidan societal securitization ritual can be equated to large-group rituals, which, according to Vamik Volkan, 'can be divided usefully into two general categories, first rituals that occur within a society that do not involve an active relationship with a contemporary "other" large group, and alternatively rituals that occur through, and depend upon, the interaction with an opposing or enemy large group, usually a neighbour or an "unwanted" subgroup, such as a minority ethnic group within a state. In practice, however, it is difficult to make a definite distinction between the two types. Both are intensified or modified when large-group regression sets in, and thus provide the foundation of signs and symptoms of large-group regression' (Volkan, 2004: 90)

Moreover, all the Maidan events, and the artistic productions flowing from them, are constructed on an idea of nationhood, and 'nationhood is not a question of some abstract, analytical category applied to various cases in which it fits more or less nicely. Objective factors such as language or location might be involved in the idea of national identity, but it nevertheless remains a political and personal choice to identify with some community by emphasizing some trait in contrast to other available historical or contemporary ties. Threats to identity are thus always a question of the construction of something as threatening some "we"' (Buzan, Waever and de Wilde, 1998: 120). Once a community, in this case the Ukrainian people, who participated and supported the Maidan, sensed that their identity, and the construction of their identity, was under existential threat, they activated what is called the securitization process. The new-Ukrainian identity became the referent object of the securitization process which was under existential threat. For Buzan, Waever, and de Wilde, securitization is 'a more extreme version of politicization. In theory, any public issue can be located on the spectrum ranging from non-politicized (meaning the state does not deal with it and it is not in any other way made an issue of public debate and decision), through being politicized (meaning the issue is part of public policy, requiring government decision and resource allocations or, more rarely, some other form of communal governance), to being fully securitized (meaning the issue is presented as an existential threat, requiring emergency measures and justifying action outside the normal bounds of political procedure)' (Buzan, Waever, and de Wilde, 1999: 23-24).

However, the process of securitization is more than a speech act (Buzan, Waever, and de Wilde, 1998: 24-26; Balzacq 2011) through which an issue is presented as an existential threat requiring emergency measures and justifying actions outside the bounds of 'normal' political procedure (Buzan, Waever, and de Wilde, 1998: 23-24). It is rather 'an articulated assemblage of practices whereby heuristic artefacts (metaphors, policy tools, image repertoires, analogies, stereotypes, emotions, etc.) are contextually mobilized by a securitizing actor, who works to prompt an audience to build a coherent network of implications (feelings, sensations, thought, and intuitions) about the critical vulnerability of a referent object that concurs with the securitizing actor's reasons for choices and actions, by investing the referent object with such an aura of unprecedented threatening complexion that a customized policy must be undertaken immediately to block its development' (Balzacq, 2011: 3). Securitization is a linguistic event, a pronouncement or linguistic move which establishes a change in the status of an issue or relationship, but it is not only a linguistic event, and it is frequently also material and structural.

Moreover, 'the securitization process is a "sacral" political spectacle which is fabricated and performed as a ritual' (Ercolani, 2016: 46). It is through this ritual process that the Maidan, as a social myth, acquired its sacredness, that 'sacredness that mainly distinguishes myth from all other collective imaginaries' (Bouchard, 2017: 25). At the same time, as the informants-interviewees all stressed, the Maidan was a rite of passage 'which accompanies a passage from one situation to another or from one cosmic or social world to another' (Van Gennep, 1960:10). It is significant that all informants-interviewees came out of that experience completely changed: Neda Nedjana even spoke of 'catharsis' to define what she had lived in Maidan. And everybody interviewed referred to these experiences as the power of the 'Spirit of Maidan' (дух), which brought together as their essence an 'animal symbolicum' (Cassirer, 1972) and a 'homo ritualis' (LisónTolosana, 2012), all of them born again as 'homines Maidan'.

Maidan was therefore a great ritual which here is termed the 'Maidan societal securitization ritual'. It creates a sense of common security and at the same time redefines what might count as a security threat to the society as a whole. One part is engaging with its spirit. A further part is taking part once it has been established, in particular to visit the museum (in person or online) and experience it. The Maidan societal securitization ritual, in its performance, created two opposite forces (Ercolani, 2016: 53-58): centripetal and centrifugal.

One part of that ritual was the actual creation of the museum. The centripetal force, for its character of urgency, emergency, and existential threat represented by the police and government attacks, and the killing of demonstrators, participated in the reinforcement and in the recreation of the identity of all the participants.

The centrifugal force of the rite of Maidan generated that spark (Canetti, 1972), and/or social (and religious) electricity that make an audience to be called to play not a game, but an active emotional-interpretative role, because this situation is inherently dramatic. The participants, first, 'not only do things, they show themselves and others what they are doing or have done: actions take on a reflexive and performed-for-an-audience aspect' (Schechner, 2003: 186), they also crystallize as a mass, leaving aside what is a formless and shapeless quality (Canetti, 1972); the partecipants are transformed into partecipants-mass. Second, they spread fear-anxiety and produced emotional contagion which created 'collective effervescence' by which 'within a crowd moved by a common passion, we become susceptible to feelings and actions of which we are incapable on our own' (Durkheim, 2001: 157). Third, they transmitted an alarm signal which participated in the construction of imagined communities (Anderson, 2006) through its language. Fourth, they recruited subjects among the individuals, or transformed individuals into subjects through an operation called 'interpellation', which refers to the process by which people, when 'hailed' by discourse, recognize themselves in that hailing (Althusser,1988: 55). 'Interpellation assumes that different representations of the world incorporate patterns of identity and ways of functioning in theworld, which are located within different power relations and which make different interests possible. Concrete individuals come to identify with these subject positions and the representations in which they appear. As subjects identify with them, the power relations and interests entailed in discourse are naturalized and these representations seem to reflect the world as it really is' (Fierke, 2007: 86).

Moreover, the use of symbols in the ritual contributes to the creation of an 'aesthetic experience' (Svasek, 2007: 10). They produce the 'distribution of the sensible', which, according to Rancière, is the law governing the sensible order that parcels out places and forms of participation in a common world by first establishing the modes of perception within which these are inscribed, and which produces a system of self-evident facts of perception based on a set horizons and modalities of what is visible and audible as well as what can be said, thought, made, or done. The 'distribution' refers both to form of inclusion and to form of exclusion. The 'sensible' refers to what is 'aistheton' (sensible) or capable of being apprehended by the senses (Rancière, 2014: 89).

In conclusion, the Maidanization process is the combination of the Maidan mythification process (Bouchard, 2017) with the Maidan societal securitization ritual (Ercolani, 2016), it produced the 'Spirit of Maidan' (дух), participated in the production of the aura of the art of Maidan, and it presented itself as an antagonist socio-cultural paradigm-habitus of reference for the construction of a post-Maidan Ukrainian identity. And Glib Viches made it very clear how the Spirit of Maidan is present in the art of Maidan: 'what I want to say is that the objects I collected from Maidan, even if people can consider them as garbage, in reality they are relics, they testify and embody the Spirit of Maidan (дух)'.

4.4.   Conclusion

This chapter has unwrapped the concept of the Spirit of Maidan pointing to its specific characteristics. It has given an account of the theory of the Maidanization process, which is the result of the combination of the Maidan mythification process with the Maidan Societal Securitization ritual, and so produced the Spirit of Maidan. The 'Maidanization process' assembled an antagonist socio-cultural paradigm-habitus of reference for the construction of the post-Maidan Ukrainian identity (homo Maidan), and a new cultural paradigm in the Ukrainian revolution of Dignity. It has also demonstrated the value of the theoretical scheme which this book has adopted in making sense of the complex interactions which have shaped the transition from a soviet inclined culture to something different and potentially liberating. Whether or not the Spirit of Maidan successfully achieves that full liberating transition remains in question, but the potentiality is evidently already there. The next chapter will focus on the main case study of this academic work, the Maidan Museum.

5
The Maidan Museum

5.1. Introduction

The National Memorial to the Heavenly Hundred Heroes and Revolution of Dignity Museum, also known as the Maidan Museum, is the only national museum devoted to collecting, exhibiting, interpreting and disseminating the stories of the struggles of Ukrainians for national independence, human rights, individual freedoms and dignity. In doing this, it is equally important in memorializing the 107 protestors who were killed. Since its inception, the representatives of Maidan Museum have collected more than two thousand artefacts, documents, photos and testimonies. They have formed the base for the National Memorial to the Heavenly Hundred Heroes and Revolution of Dignity Museum. In creating the Museum, its leadership consulted with internationally reputed museologists before arranging a series of exhibition projects in Ukraine and abroad. They visited a number of European museums to profit from their experiences, in particular as regards the creation of 'museums of memory' and associated challenges.

The mission of the Maidan Museum can best be evidenced by a review of its activities, which are already clear from the earlier discussion. But to summarise, they include:

1. The commemoration and preservation of memory of those affected by the clashes, as well as of activists and protest participants.
2. Collecting, studying, and popularizing testimonies about the events that took place during the Revolution of Dignity.
3. Conceptualizing the phenomenon of Maidan, as well as the civil and political transformations and social innovations caused by it.
4. The presentation and promotion of knowledge about the struggle of Ukrainian people for their rights and dignity in the context of the world movement for freedom.

5. Stimulating rethinking and renewed awareness of universal and national values, identity, and of the moral and spiritual challenges that were made relevant by the Revolution of Dignity, and so stimulating critical thinking and innovative creativity.

6. Supporting the establishment of the civil society in Ukraine and the creation of democratic platforms, whose goal is to find ways to develop and support the civil practices initiated by Maidan.

The Maidan Museum (2021) has over four thousand items in its collections: artefacts; oral history; works of art, including songs, poems, fiction, ornamental and fine arts, photos, audio and video recordings, leaflets, publications, and documents.

After an open competition, from September Dr Ihor Poshyvailo has served as Director General of the Revolution of Dignity Museum. On September 14, 2017, Kyiv City Council Decision No 9/3016 allocated the land plot for the construction, operation and maintenance of the Memorial and Museum Complex on Heavenly Hundred Heroes Alley. However, at the moment (autumn 2021), the Museum of Maidan is still a work-in-progress. It does not possess its proper building, but has at its disposal the 'Information and Exhibition Center of the Maidan Museum', which is a space where one can learn about the course of the Euromaidan, get information about the route of Revolution of the Dignity, order excursions, bring objects for the exhibition, leave memories about the revolution, and learn about the activities of the National Memorial Complex of the Heroes of the Heavenly Hundred — Museum of the Revolution of the Dignity. This information centre is located in the city centre of Kyiv in 120 square metres and two floors of the new House of Trade Unions. On the first floor, there is a temporary exhibition 'Towards Freedom!'. Visitors are fully immersed in the atmosphere of the actions on the Maidan by the help of multimedia and through the narratives of participants, which are made available in an audio presentation. On the second floor, visitors are able to examine the map of Maidan Square and its area, where key events of the Revolution, barricades and central buildings are shown.

This chapter extends the earlier arguments by presenting interview material from important conversations the author held with Dr Ihor Poshyvailo (General Director of the Maidan Museum) and Dr Kateryna Romanova (Head of Research Department of the Maidan Museum). Their testimony is the best possible evidence of the nature, meaning, and mission of the Maidan Museum, and of their own experience during the Maidan events.

5.2. The Maidan Museum according to Dr Ihor Poshyvailo

After an initial meeting with Dr Ihor Poshyvailo (figure 44), in November 2016, he was interviewed at the 'Ivan Honchar Museum' (Kyiv, Ukraine), and then again in June 2019. He is an ethnologist, museologist, cultural activist, and art curator. He was awarded his PhD in History by the National Academy of Sciences of Ukraine. Currently he holds the position of Director General of the National Memorial to the Heavenly Hundred Heroes and Revolution of Dignity Museum (Maidan Museum) in Kyiv. He is Vice-Chair of the ICOM-DRMC Committee. He is author of the award-winning academic book 'Phenomenology of Pottery' as well as numerous articles on the arts and culture, cultural heritage preservation, cultural emergency management, presentation of conflicted history, and policies of historical memory. He is also the author and editor of a number of academic books on traditional culture and disaster risk management.

Both interviews in 2016 and 2019 with Dr Poshyvailo focused on four issues:

(1) The concepts of artivism, art as resistance, emancipation, consciousness. 'Art/artivism can help the individual (like the case of the demonstrators in Maidan square) to produce a discourse of emancipation and to help the individual become conscious of himself in pursuit of that goal.'

(2) The Maidan Square demonstrations from an artistic perspective, namely the production in the Maidan Square of articrafts conveying symbols that were used and reused.

(3) The analysis of the events in the Maidan Square through an anthropological lens, viz. symbols and rituals as parts of the demonstrations and the events and forming, one might argue, a rite of passage, a ritual of initiation.

(4) The meaning and function of the Maidan Museum.

Figure 44. IhorPoshyvailo. (Photo credit: G. Ercolani, 2016)

One of the very original ideas which emerged from this first interview was the concept of the Maidan Museum as a 'platform', focused on art, culture, and social. This concept makes the Maidan Museum an active agent of cultural mediation (Peters, 2020: 110-111).

According to Ihor 'the Maidan Museum will be a different model of museum, not like the Museum of Traditional Culture also in Kiyv. The idea of a platform is a concept much widerthan only concentrating on culture and the museum's first exhibition after the Maidan events was a combination of different initiatives: artistic and social. The exhibition was presented in the National Art

Museum with Vlodko Kaufman, a famous artist from Lviv, as curator. It was about freedom, Maidan, and art. The main idea was the creativity of freedom, the core artistic expression of Maidan. There was noframework, but only pure intuition. Art can be a platform that can be understood from different angles. We have the Maidan angle and the anti-Maidan angle. There were other angles presently being examined as part over the overarching demand of for whom the museum should be created, and the nature of the message it should be carrying. We therefore seek the testimonials of the families of the heroes (Heaven's Hundred Heroes), too. At the demonstrations (Maidan events) there were a lot of active students, who were not only thinking about art, but about social change, political change. Therefore, different issues conflate. As regardsthe platform, it should be a platform for reactivating public initiatives. For us it was interesting, on one hand we had art expression, art as a means of protest, art as one of the forms of protest, and on the other hand we had the bursts social activism, where people became voluntaries, especially in Ukraine. After the implosion of the Soviet Union, people became very passive, politically and socially, and Maidan showed that this was not the truth. The general mentality was to care about one's own house, one's own garden. Therefore, Maidan and the previous Orange Revolution showed that citizens could become social active, could believe in their own force, and that they could change the country. But first of all, they had to change themselves. As specifically regards art, he noted that art has a special place in Ukraine, and that art museums and artistic realizations all have a special importance in Ukraine. The artists, in general, feel the future, the need of change. Artists in Ukraine have always understood, even in the past, that there was a social change. They were capable to define revolutions and sometime to name of the revolution, even before the revolution unfolded itself. So, in Ukraine artists are in the vanguard of changes. Another important role of art was to build communities, and to create messages, especially to outside Ukraine, to USA i.e., because they were depicting the reality of Maidan. This was a reaction to official media depiction of the protestors (right wing people, vandals, wild football supporters, etc) but the intellectuals showed the reality by means of art'.

The topic of the Maidan events as a rite/ritual of passage emerges in the words of Ihor. There was a 'before the Maidan events', and an 'after the Maidan events' phase, and through this ritual people became emancipated and conscious. The Maidan became a ritual of initiation where the protestors, who embodied both the 'animal symbolicum' (Cassirer, 1972) and 'homo ritualis' (Lisón Tolosana, 2012), were transformed by the Spirit of Maidan into the 'homo Maidan'. Maidan originated the 'homo Maidan'. And the arts played a very important role because they created a space in which the actions took place.

For Ihor 'the major space of art was created though the mean of "Yolka" (Christmas tree). The President of Ukraine (Yanukovych) used the pretext to erect the "Yolka' in order to destroy the Maidan demonstration camp. But the students stopped the construction of this "Yolka", so that the construction was not finished, and they transformed the empty construction site into a space of intense narration, as it gradually became decorated with flags, slogans, banners, posters, and it was changed in the most democratic art space. This was for me the first artistic production. Then, there was a group of artists from Lviv, who painted elements of "shopka" (a nativity scene; "shopka" is a traditional portable nativity scene used to represent nativity and other figures in a puppet form), because it was Christmas time. And they brought it with them from Lviv to Maidan. This work is present in the Maidan Museum collections. They are a big construction of nativity scene, painted in nice way, and originally installed it in Maidan area. In this way, the artists responsible for the "shopka" provided an art work, which carried — and still carries — a core part of Ukrainian culture. Some artists brought their paintings to Maidan, while other professional artists organized pop up exhibitions, putting their paints on the wall in Maidan. A lot of photographers displayed their photographs as well as a lot of posters. We had a lot of exhibitions everywhere. There were installations, too, like a cage where the president of Ukraine was depicted inside, with a space for judges. All these artists were expressing their feelings and their furiousness against the Ukrainian president for not signing the EU agreement. They even organized an event called Artists Barbican (there were barricades painted as art objects). There were a lot of installation exhibitions. And they published a catalogue for the event. They were the first to publish a very catalogue with concepts and explanations. They collected objects, they had limited space, they were inviting people, they organized exhibitions by prominent artists, and the exhibition travelled around Europe and USA. Other premises used by the artists were the building of the former Lenin Museum in Europe Square, now "Ukraine House". It was taken by the protestors, then the police came, and they destroyed everything. This was one of the temporary places of our Maidan Museum. There was another active initiative called the Artistic Squadron, professional artists who painted shields, helmets, and lamps. And this was a kind of exhibition. They painted posters for "yolka". And when the police arrived, they destroyed almost everything. I was there after two hours of police destruction, and I was able to preserve some objects, like shields in wood painted by some artists. There were murals, which now only survive in few places (Ivan Franko), another one with our political leader (Timoshenko) with binocular and the European flag. Where there is this last mural, was the border of the demonstrators' area. In front of the National Art Museum, there is a catapult, and this is a piece of art, not an effective weapon. We talk about visual art, but in a broad sense, because there were people who made performance and played music, too. Our museum organized a huge flash mob on Christmas day with music, concert, dance, and singing'.

The Maidan Museum, which was still a work in progress in 2016 and still again in 2019, is at the centre of a political controversy. Apparently, back in 2016, the local political authorities supported the initiative. The situation, however, has not improved. In 2016 this was the opinion of Ihor: 'the Maidan Museum was originated by a public initiative. That same year, in January 2016, the Museum was officially funded by the government. The Maidan Museum is run by the state, and it has been recognised as a National Museum by the President of Ukraine. Therefore, it is a national museum ran by the state. But the problem remains the premises. To have premises, a location, in order to make not only a museum, but a place of memory, and to study and disseminate the ways of preserving memory. And such premises depend on the political will of the President and of our City Mayor. Because the land belongs to Kyiv, and there is not too much free land in the centre of Kyiv, therefore, the question is quite problematic. At the moment, after one year, there has been no progress on the topic. Then, is hard to say if the government sincerely supportsthe Maidan Museum or not. Their support is slow, and it is not effective. The general idea of a museum structure is to have a memorial complex. It should consist in three parts: a memorial space (territory, memory; preserve memory, murals); a classic museum; and a platform (the House of Freedom). It should be a space in the centre of Kyiv for people, for public initiatives. Now, for example, we are thinking about the new concept of museum, a museum that reaches outside its physical walls. Going back to talk about art expression, we try to preserve the as much as possible of the objects produced by creative people, which are considered as objects of art'.

Talking about symbolic elements of the post-Maidan Ukrainian identity, the one this author defined as the 'homo Maidan', the Maidan Museum has an important role in preserving and promoting these elements, which are summarized in the concept of Ukrainian culture and the Ukrainian national flag. Already the totality of the 2019 interviews confirms these relations, and the Maidan Museum from its beginning has acted in this sense: to preserve and to promote.

Ihor has elucidated all these points: 'I do agree that these two elements (Ukrainian culture and Ukrainian National Flag) can be symbols of the Maidan events and of the post Maidan Ukrainian identity. Even in the barricades we saw a lot of these elements, and even the symbols of the "Cossack Mamai". However, at the same time there were typical folk art that you see in the Ukrainian villages. These folk themes were depicted on the demonstrators' tents. There were images of Taras Shevchenko everywhere. Even the way the Maidan was self-organized was like a Cossack village, where people took decision in a general assembly. And the people started to use even Cossack terminology, people used to come on

Sunday to "viche maidan" ("viche" is a Cossack term for square). Talking about the Ukrainian national flag, I do completely agree, because even during Maidan, when Crimea was annexed to Russia (March 2014), our museum organized an exhibition (April 2014) supporting the Crimean Tatar, especially Crimean artists who escaped to Ukraine.One artist, Rustem Skibin, collected a lot of Tatar objects and created a house in Crimea, with all this Tatar stuff. And when Crimea was in danger, he took a lot of objects and came to Kyiv, and we organized an exhibition with his material and with other Crimean artists who escaped. And during an interview I had with Rustem, talking about the flag, during the opening of the exhibition, it was very emotional, and he said that before Maidan the Ukrainian flag to Crimean Tatars represented nothing, it was not their flag, but after Maidan, when he saw how flags were neglected by anti-Maidan Russian supporters, this flag became their own flag. Even for the Tatars, the Ukrainian flag became special. There were even special rituals for people killed in Maidan, the coffins were taken to the main stage and these people sang a special song (a cappella song from Lviv). This was a folk farewell song ("Plyvekacha"), a very sad song, which became the hymn for the killed people. Maidan was a context, made out of everything. And even this exclamation "Slava Ukraine" (Glory to Ukraine) was used by the politicians. Even before to say "hello" the politicians were saying 'Slava Ukraine' and the people were replying "Glory to the Heroes". It was used everywhere and at different levels. Everybody started to use these expressions. It showed who was sympathetic to the events.

For Ihor: 'the Maidan produced a language by itself, its own language, and rituals, and non-verbal as well as verbal language. Examples of non-verbal language were to wear a ribbon with the colours of the Ukrainian flag, the meaning of which was that you were sympathizing with the Maidan demonstrators, and this practice was very dangerous at the beginning. People were attaching these ribbons everywhere, on their clothes, on their bags. People who were coming to Maidan were putting on ribbons, but on their way back home it could be dangerous because the anti-Maidan people could attack them. There is the story of a young lady who was wearing this ribbon, she was on a bus, and an old lady approached her and asked her to remove the ribbon. The young girl started an animated conversation with the old lady, but the old lady said that she was supporting Maidan, but that to wear the ribbon was very dangerous. She was talking for her security, because it was dangerous to show the ribbon around. Coming back to the topic of language and identity, even people who were living in the Russian speaking area of Ukraine started to speak Ukrainian. This created a problem in families, faced with the emergence of a Ukrainian identity and the use of its language. They were speaking about the policy from above, because there was an ukrainization of the country. But it was from above, and this already started in the 1960. And it did not work. The political power was saying you have to speak Ukrainian, but the people were not following. Maybe outside of their homes, they spoke Ukrainian, but inside the family they were continuing to use Russian. But after the Maidan events, everybody started to speak Ukrainian. For example, there were some incidents that took place during Maidan events in some coffee shops run by Russian companies. People were going there and ordering in Ukrainian and the waiter were not serving them, saying we don't understand. And confrontations started. Therefore, people started to boycott Russian products, even in our supermarkets. And, as a form of social initiative products were identified, and the ones classified as Russian were not bought. If you were buying Russian products it meant that you were supporting the Russian aggression against Crimea. Therefore, in Maidan there were the constructions of the "we" vs. "the others". But "the others" were not Russia, but Putin. And much more intensely after Crimea was annexed. We had a lot of people from Russia, from Belorussia, supporting Ukrainian Maidan. Coming back to the topic of exhibition, there was an exhibition by the National Art Museum at the residence (that he had abandoned) of President Yanukovych, of his belongings. This was done in order to show to the public the mentality of these people. Even Viktor Yushchenko, former President of Ukraine 2005-2010, tried to build up a typical Ukrainian village, not far from Kyiv, but everything is not high quality and the material collected is not good too'.

Now, in 2019, the shape of the Maidan Museum is clearer. As an institution (still without an official building) it is a memorial and museum complex which consists of three main conceptual, organizational and functional elements: Memorial to the Heavenly Hundred Heroes and (past), Revolution of Dignity Museum (present) and House of Freedom (future). In perspective it is envisioned as a national centre of freedom and human rights. And its purpose, according to Ihor, is 'to provide a profound response to the challenges and possibilities in presenting and interpreting significant national events by creating a modern place of a new type, a place of living stories and true testimonies, a repository of collective memory and a laboratory of its reinterpretation, a platform for public dialogue, common ground and action.We aim to create a museum of dialogue, to become "a safe place for challenging ideas". It will provide an informative response to various challenges and possibilities — to commemorate our heroes, to rethink the complicated history, to present significant national events. The Maidan Museum purpose is driven from its mission statement: to preserve, present and spread, in Ukraine and abroad, the history of Ukrainians struggles for national and personal freedom, dignity, human and civil rights, as well as revitalization of the public initiatives for establishing democratic society in Ukraine'.

Therefore, the Maidan Museum is becoming more than a simple 'building', an active agent of the cultural policy of Ukraine, and its mission is evident in all the activities which are organised by the Museum, as exhibitions, gatherings, memorial services, conferences, all of them carrying the 'mark' of the Maidan Museum. As a consequence, the very Maidan Museum, as a cultural mediator, has become a brand perpetuating the Spirit of Maidan. Ihor confirms this point, saying that the 'Euromaidan itself was the event which made Ukraine visible worldwide and became a kind of a brand. In this way the Maidan Museum is an ambitious project which envisioned creating of something new and important not only to Ukrainians and post-Soviet nations, but other countries as well. Maidan's ideals and objectives were connected to universal values of freedom, human rights, dignity, honesty, solidarity, openness. So we try to make the very process of themuseum a creation corresponding to these values. Its strategic assets are focused on the interests and values of the citizens, since it is all about the memory that museum is trying to preserve, the people who are honoured there, the collections, the ideas that are being generated, and the reputation that is being protected'.

In conclusion, Ihor unfolds the reasons why it is important to have the Maidan Museum: 'first and foremost—because the Maidan Museum becomes a part of a strong infrastructure of historical and national memories which will not allow the manipulation of Euromaidan facts and processes, positive experience and historical importance, peoples' lives, values, aspirations and hopes, will not admit historical and social amnesia. It is in fact the only institution in Ukraine to present and promote the knowledge about the contemporary struggle of Ukrainian people for their rights and dignity in the context of the world movement for freedom. It will stimulate critical thinking and innovative creativity, rethinking and awareness of universal and national values, identity, moral and spiritual challenges that were brought to discourse and made relevant by the Revolution of Dignity. And finally, it is an effective tool to disseminate knowledge about Ukraine's identity, for the establishment of the civil society in Ukraine,and the creation of democratic platforms, whose goal is to find ways to develop and support the civil practices initiated by Maidan'.

In a world of fake news and carefully curated misinformation, having a distinctive centre of gravity which maintains the narratives of the experiences of Maidan is a most important defence against the opponents of Ukrainian identity and the enemies of the struggles of those who created the Revolution of 2013-14.

5.3. Visiting the Maidan Museum with Dr Kateryna Romanova

I met Dr Kateryna Romanova (figure 51) at the Maidan Museum Office, 16 Lypska Street, Kyiv (Ukraine). Kateryna Romanova holds a PhD in Historical Sciences (her specialities are ethnography, ethnology, and anthropology), from the Peter the Great Museum of Anthropology and Ethnography, Saint-Petersburg, Russia. She is the author of monographs and scientific publications in Ukrainian and of foreign editions, in particular 'Archives of Ukraine', 'Rossica Romana', and 'Harvard Ukrainian Studies'. Dr Romanova is the Head of the Research Department of the Maidan Museum. Our interview took place on June 18th, 2019, and in practice was a visit to the Maidan Museum archives. Kateryna showed me part of the objects preserved in the temporary archive of the Maidan Museum, and recalled the story behind some important objects of art.

Kateryna: 'a lot of the works of art that we have in the Maidan Museum were collected in the Independence Square (Maidan Nezalezhnosti) and sometime we do not know the artist who produced them. However, every one of these objects has been catalogued. Talking about the groups of artists which were present at the Maidan demonstration, I can mention the following: "Art Hundred", they started drawing and painting on the shield. One of the artists, who now lives in USA, was Kateryna Tkachenko. She produced the following shield titled "Blooming Heart" (figure 45).

Figure 45. Painted shield 'Blooming Heart' by Kateryna Tkachenko.
(Photo credit: G. Ercolani, 2019)

Other shields were decorated with angels, or reproduced some birds, for example doves and, crows that carry meanings like the following shield (figure 46).

Figure 46. Painted shield, courtesy of the Maidan Museum

It is important to observe that on a lot of the shields and other art works one finds the "tryzub", the trident that is the national symbol of Ukraine, and likewise the blue and yellow colours which are the same of the Ukrainian flag.

A case in point is the work of Yulia Ovnachenko (figure 47).

Figure 47. Detail of painted shield by Yulia Ovnachenko, courtesy of the Maidan Museum

The symbol of the "tryzub" acquired a new meaning, during the Maidan events, and now, after the Maidan Revolution it represents the Ukrainian State nd the convergence of European values and Ukrainian values. Another group of artists which were present in Maidan was "Artistic Barbican". They established their area in the city administrative offices. "Barbican" means a fortified outpost or gateway, such as an outer defence of a city or castle, or any tower situated over a gate or bridge for defensive purposes. This group of artists and poets started as an artistic initiative, but afterwards they joined the confrontation/demonstration against the riot police

(Berkut). At the Maidan Museum we keep various works produced there, which we recuperated. We have here at the Maidan Museum an embroidery work by Ivan Semesyuk (figure 48) that is against Putin, along with other art objects from the same group. The message is: "Putin– khuilo!" (Ukrainian: "Путін—хуйло", commonly translated as 'Putin is a "dickhead").

Figure 48. 'Putin– khuilo!' by Ivan Semesyuk, courtesy of the Maidan Museum

From Maidan Square we brought a lot of material, which we are still cataloguing. There were no artists in the Trade Union building during the Revolution of Dignity. But after the fire in that building, Tatyana Cheprasova found many items from the Maidan participants and handed them over to our museum. She painted some of these items later. The items were decorated helmets and decorated shields. The symbols used were the "tryzub", flowers, and words as 'Slava Ukrayni!' (Glory to Ukraine!) from the national poet Taras Shevchenko. Other things that we gathered were armour chest. And painted helmets like these ones produced Tatyana Cheprasova (figure 49).

Figure 49. Painted helmets by Tatyana Cheprasova. (Photo credit: G. Ercolani, 2019)

What emerges from a lot of these art works is that the artists had different levels of technical mastery. The motivation behind this work was to document what was going on, but at the same time we now have a portrait of the participants in Maidan.

One characteristic symbol of Maidan was the Ukrainian flag together with the European Union flag. The "tryzub" symbol became attached to the Spirit of Maidan: for the people working for the government, the tryzub is the symbol of authority; whilst for the protestors of Maidan the tryzub means to defend the Ukranian people. Another image used as a symbol is that of tyres. Tyres were burned by the protesters in order to hide themselves from the police, in order not to be visible. And, if we talk about icons and religious images of the Maidan, they are similar in style to Ukrainian folk icons or home icons; this, for instance, is the case of the use of the image of Saint Michael (figure 50, 51), who is the protector of Kyiv.

Figure 50. Detail of painted shield with Saint Michael, courtesy of the Maidan Museum

Figure 51. Kateryna Romanova showing a Saint Michael icon.
(Photo credit: G. Ercolani, 2019)

Therefore, we have the image of Saint Michael and the tryzub (figure 51), and this icon become the icon of the protector of the Kiev protesters. Through a lot of works of art, one senses that the protesters were fighting against the forces of Evil, like in the work of Vasyl Korchynskyi (figure 52). This again embodies the sacral quality which many of the Maidan works enshrine.

Figure 52. 'Maidan' by Vasyl Korchynskyi, courtesy by the Maidan Museum

Maidan definitely conveyed a new meaning to these symbols (decorated helmets, tyres, etc.). During the Maidan revolution a symbolic discourse was constructed and fabricated; I consider the Maidan revolution a work in progress (2019) and we are still investigating these events.

If you look at the place close to Maidan Square, where we have the picture of the killed people you will always see a helmet and an icon. In my opinion the symbolic framework of Maidan is represented by: the "tryzub", the tyre, the decorated helmet, Saint Michael, and the decorated shields.

As regards religious symbols: everyday there were religious services in Maidan. They were short services performed by different religious observances. The Church of Moscow was not present in Maidanbecause it did not support the Maidan events.

A particularly interesting symbol was the Cossack hair style: "oseledets" (Ukrainian: оселедець, herring) is an element of a traditional Ukrainian Cossack haircut. And the image of the national poet Taras Shevchenko.

Another important aspect related to the twin concepts of Maidan and identity is the experience of the artist Ola Rondiak (figure 53, 54) who lives in USA. This is interesting because we are talking about Ukranian diaspora people. For her the Maidan revolution represents the "founding myth" of the identity of the new Ukrainian people'.

Figure 53. Work by Ola Rondiak, courtesy of the Maidan Museum

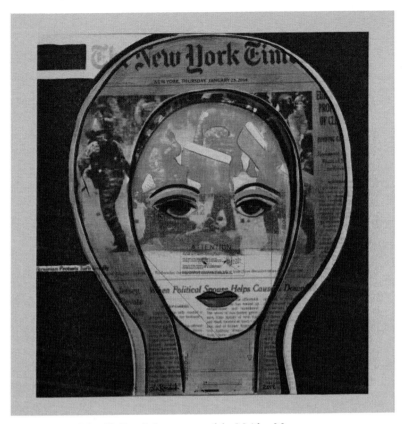

Figure 54. Work by Ola Rondiak, courtesy of the Maidan Museum

5.4.   The Maidan Museum's Mimesis: Make-Feel

The Maidan Museum frames the whole of the Revolution of Dignity events. In doing this it has invested in an original implementation of the concept of mimesis which has been tied to the emotions of the Maidan experience. In this particular characteristic it is possible to appreciate the fact that here a different kind of mimesis has been realized. Whilst the term mimesis (from classical Greek: to imitate) has been used in aesthetic or artistic theory to refer to the attempt to imitate or reproduce reality, the Maidan Museum has implemented a mimesis which aims to 'make-feel' the emotions triggered by the Revolution of Dignity. At the same time, it is always a project to imitate a reality, or perhaps to define a reality, as a serious and possibly difficult endeavour, rather than a frivolous 'imitation'.

If in art galleries and museums, the expository montage operates as a translation (Tejeda Martin, 2006 - see also the earlier discussion of translation in this text and in Farrands' Foreword), the Maidan Museum has incorporated in its expository space places outside the very 'building' of the museum which are part of its artistic and revolutionary discourse. In this way, it has converted urban areas which could have been classified as non-places before the Maidan events into anthropological and emotional places. The category of 'non-place', refers according to Augé (2009) to anthropological spaces of transience where human beings remain anonymous, and that do not hold enough significance to be regarded as 'places' in their anthropological definition. Non-places can be anonymous urban areas, shopping malls, airports, motorways and other places of transition where those who pass through lose their identities. The perception of a non-place is strictly personal and it is based on personal relations with a specific place. The transformed Maidan space is both private and public, but it carries multiple meanings and identities.

However, the dramatic Maidan events have transformed urban non-places into anthropological places in which even the collective perception recalls the killing of people. In these places, the demonstrators of the Revolution of Dignity met their death. They have been killed there. And these places are part of expository space and artistic discourse of the Maidan Museum. Figure 55 shows the locations of the National Revolution of Dignity Museum and the places of the Revolution of Dignity and the whole of this emotional area is the 'make feel' space of the Maidan Museum.

Regularly, personnel of the Maidan Museum organize commemorative celebrations and memorial service in these areas in remembrance of the Heroes of the Heavenly Hundred. In this performative way, the museum: (1) has reduced the frontier between art and life (Tejeda Martin, 2006: 60); (2) has converted the expository space as part of the art works (Tejeda Martin, 2006: 62); and (3) has transformed the whole of its space into a sacred area. The whole of the expository space of the Maidan Museum becomes a component of the art works without which they are radically transformed. 'The meaning of the objects is reconstructed from the exhibition strategies, from their apparently innocent visual disposition. After all, exposure is language and organization of knowledge' (Tejeda Martin, 2006: 99). Therefore, the visitor to the Maidan Museum experiences visually and emotionally the Revolution of Dignity, because in visiting the dramatic places of the revolution he/she feels the Spirit of Maidan.

Figure 56, 57, 58, 59, from the Archive of the Maidan Museum, shows the extent of the Museum, currently located in a number of different sites which it is hoped will be brought together in a single all-embracing site.

Locations of the National Revolution of Dignity Museum

1 Stands «Heaven Hundreds» and «Revolution of Dignity» (Yevropeyska (European) Square / Khreschatyk street, 2

2 Stands «Heaven Hundreds» (Mykhailo Hrushevsky street, 1)

3 Information and Exhibition Center of the Maidan Museum (Maydan Nezalezhnosti (Independence square), 18/2)

4 Street exhibition and educational space «M²: Maidan. Memorial. Museum» (from November 2019 to April 2021) (Heroyv Nebesnoyi Sotni (Heroes of Heaven Hundreds) alley, 3-5)

5 Maidan Museum Library and Protest Art Gallery (Lypska street, 16)

6 Bell of Dignity (near the Ecumenical Church of the Archangel Michael and the Ukrainian New Martyrs of the Ukrainian Greek Catholic Church, the Heroyv Nebesnoyi Sotni (Heroes of the Heavenly Hundred) alley)

7 Wall of Remembrance of the Fallen for Ukraine (Heroes of the Heavenly Hundred and Russian-Ukrainian War), St. Michael's Golden-domed Cathedral (Tryokhsviatytelska (Three Saints) street

8 Metal Exhibition Stands «Landscapes of memory» around the Independence Monument (Maydan Nezalezhnosti (Independence square))

Stands: Places of the Revolution of Dignity

9 «St. Michael's Square» (St. Michael's square)

10 «Ukrainskyi Dim» (Yevropeyska (European) square / Khreschatyk street, 2)

11 «The intersection of Heroyv Nebesnoyi Sotni alley and Khreschatyk street» (Khreschatyk Street, 7)

12 «Instytutska street» (Heroyv Nebesnoyi Sotni (Heroes of the Heavenly Hundred) alley, 6)

13 «Maydan Nezalezhnosti» (Independence square)

14 «Central post office» (Khreschatyk street, 22)

15 «Kyiv City State Administration » (Khreschatyk street, 36)

16 «1 Mykhailo Hrushevsky street» (Mykhailo Hrushevsky street, 1)

17 «6 Mykhailo Hrushevsky street. The National Art Museum of Ukraine» (Mykhailo Hrushevsky street, 6)

18 «The Trade Union Building» (Maydan Nezalezhnosti (Independence square))

19 Observation deck of Globus shopping center (Maydan Nezalezhnosti (Independence square))

20 Excursion route «Places of the Revolution of Dignity»

Figure 55. Locations of the National Revolution of Dignity Museum and Places of the Revolution of Dignity, courtesy of the Maidan Museum.

Figure 56. Commemorating the Heavenly Hundred, courtesy of the Maidan Museum

Figure 57. Commemorating the Heavenly Hundred, courtesy of the Maidan Museum

Figure 58. Commemorating the Heavenly Hundred, courtesy of the Maidan Museum

Figure 59. Commemorating the Heavenly Hundred, courtesy of the Maidan Museum

5.5.   Conclusion

This chapter has examined the Maidan Museum through the voices of the General Director and the Head of the Research Department of the Maidan Museum. Dr IhoPoshyvailo and Dr Kateryna Romanova have presented their personal experiences with the Maidan events, with the creation of the Maidan Museum, with the importance of art in the Revolution of Dignity, with the symbols of Maidan, and with the work of art produced in Maidan. What emerge from the interviews are their dedication and passion, and all their efforts to make this dream to become a reality. Even if not provided with an official building named the Maidan Museum, the social activities of the Maidan virtual museum are very numerous and they involve other people of the Museum, academics, former demonstrators, artists, poets, and other creatives, all of them interested in preserving and transmitting the message of the Maidan events. The Maidan Museum is very active in all the commemoration related to the Maidan events.

6
Conclusion

This research has analyzed and explored the topic of 'The Maidan Museum: Preserving the Spirit of Maidan'. It has approached this research through three main ontological and epistemological research questions: (1) 'What the Maidan Museum is about?'; (2) 'When we talk about Maidan and the Spirit of Maidan, we are talking about what?'; and (3) 'What is the role of art and identity discourse in Maidan?'. And the research has attempted to answer all three questions, drawing on extensive field research and a wide range of interviews with key participants in both the original events of Maidan Square and in founding and building the museum as a commemorative physical and virtual site.

However, it is important to remember the genealogy of this research because in order to construct a logical and thorough study, I have assembled qualitative data from academic literature as well as interpretive academic methods to set up the fieldwork experience. This led me to move to Kyiv (Ukraine), to devote several visits to my work there, and to collect first-hand experiences.

During my first visit in 2016, I had the possibility to walk around the places that are part of the psychogeography of the Maidan events, to mix with local people that visited the same place in order to remember the bloody events, to have contact with an artistic organization, 'Izolyatsia', which as a platform for cultural initiatives promotes the work of young Ukrainian and foreign artists. It was during one of my visits to 'Izolyatsia' that Ms. Ksiu Kyrychenko (IP Rights & Fundraising Lead at Izolyatsia) mentioned to me the project of the Maidan Museum and arranged a contact with Dr IhorPoshyvailo (Director of the Maidan Museum). From that conversation, an interview with Ihor followed, and I visited the place where the majority of objects collected from the Maidan were stored. A contact was then established with the

Maidan Museum and after email exchange started between me and Ihor.

A second visit to Kyiv (2019) was part of an internship offered by the Maidan Museum. There I had the possibility to enter in the 'meaning of Maidan' through the experiences of the informants-interviewees whose words have formed such an importantn basis for the analysis argued here. They included Ihor Poshyvailo (Director Maidan Museum), Oles Kromplias (artist, photographer and war correspondent), Ekateryna Romanova (Head of the Research Department, Maidan Museum), Tatyana Cheprasova (artist, painter), Taras Kompanichenko (artist, musician), Oleksander Ivanovych Melnyk (artist, painter), Ivan Semesyuk (artist, poet, musician author), Sasha Komyakhov (artist, freelance illustrator), Yuriy Gruzinov (documentary cinema operator, winner of the Shevchenko Prize in 2018), Neda Nedjana (playwright and director), Yulia Ovcharenko (artist, illustrator), Valery Hladunets (folklorist, singer, cultural manager), Glib Viches (artist, curator, lecturer in Cultural Studies), Maryna Sochenko (artist and teacher at the Ukrainian Art Academy).

As a result, I realized that the topic of the existence of the Maidan Museum had to be focused through a different perspective, while maintaining at the centre the subject of the Spirit of Maidan. I had first to define the meaning of the Maidan events, second to define the mission of the art of Maidan, and third to unfold the role of the Maidan Museum. It is not possible to talk about the Maidan Museum outside the concept and the context of what the Maidan events were, and what they represent today.

Therefore, utilizing a comparative approach in which the narrative of the Maidan events was confronted with the results of my interviews, I realized that Maidan is a 'social myth' (Bouchard, 2017), a metalanguage (Barthes, 2005), a spiritual place (Hryhorczuk, 2016), an anthropological place (Augé, 2011), an emotional field (Beatty, 2019), and a chosen trauma (Volkan, 1999, 2004, 2006; Svasek, 2005). This language may sometimes seem convoluted, but it is unavoidably so since these separate elements of social myth combine and weave around each other in the construction of the whole.

Then, focusing on the relevance of the art of Maidan, and on the interviews, I was able to identify the symbols of Maidan. This is a key element in the identity of the Maidan Museum because the art of Maidan carries aura, tension, imminence, and is a 'conceptual art', which is an essential element in the manufacturing of antagonist collective imaginaries (a concept borrowed from Bouchard, 2017). It is central to the Maidan mythification process (again, borrowing a core concept from Bouchard, 2017). It is central to the formation of social identity (a broad and frequently contentious concept, but here the text borrows specifically from Jenkins, 2014). In turn this points to the need for the clarification of the strong relationship between identity, identification and interpellation (Althusser, 1988; Ranciere, 2014). Through all these elements, I was able to shape the theory of the Maidanization process, which is the result of the combination of the Maidan mythification process with the Maidan Societal Securitization ritual, and which produced the Spirit of Maidan. The 'Maidanization process' assembled an antagonist socio-cultural paradigm-habitus of reference for the construction of the post-Maidan Ukrainian identity ('homo Maidan'), and a new cultural paradigm in the Ukrainian revolution of Dignity.

Moreover, this work has presented the voices of the General Director of the Maidan Museum and of the Head of Research Department of the Maidan Museum. Dr Ihor Poshyvailo and Dr Kateryna Romanova have presented their personal experiences with the Maidan events, with the creation of the Maidan Museum, with the importance of art in the Revolution of Dignity, with the symbols of Maidan, and with the work of art produced in Maidan. What emerge from their interviews are their dedication and passion, and their efforts to make this dream become a reality. Even if not provided with an official building named the Maidan Museum, the social activities of the Maidan virtual museum are very numerous and they involve other people of the Museum, academics, former demonstrators, artists, musicians, poets and others, all of them interested in preserving and transmitting the message of the Maidan events and the Spirit of Maidan. The

Maidan Museum is critical in the preservation of both memories and looking forward to the future.

The result of this approach has confirmed the initial hypothesis which shaped this research project, namely that the Maidan Museum is a unique and original structure safeguarding all the elements-ingredients of the 'Maidanization process', is the guardian which preserves the 'Spirit of Maidan', and is as an active agent and cultural mediator. In the latter role, the Maidan Museum plays a unique role in the definition of the Ukrainian identity, in the field of Ukrainian cultural policy, and confirms the relationship between art and politics, symbols-language, myths, ritual and identity formation.

The Maidan Museum educates, and is an active agent and cultural mediator in the context of the cultural policy in Ukraine in which the concept of identity is a contested concept with strong political repercussions. The art of Maidan which is preserved in the Museum are works which reflect the aura of the Revolution of Dignity, these objects are relics, and ex-votos of dramatic events that saw the death of innocent people. The theory elaborated here, the 'Maidanization process', focuses on the human experience which produced the Spirit of Maidan, and the Maidan Museum, with its countless activities to maintain this spirit alive.

The Maidan Museum embodies the message of the Revolution of Dignity. What is at stake in Ukraine is the future of a country, and the development of an aptitude to face this future. It opposes and confronts the spirit of the 'zombie Sovieticus', contrasting it with the energy and dreams of the 'homo Maidan'. And the Maidan Museum frames this identitarian concept of the 'homo Maidan'. Moreover, art represents for the Maidan Museum a medium to talk on traumatic issues and method of post-trauma healing.

The present research attempts to consolidate and inspire future research into the museum collection, analysis, presentation and dissemination of art objects representing the strength of art in shaping identity. This, as expressed by Mesch (2013: 206), is because 'artists will remain active in generating new meanings. The realm of art stimulates new ways of thinking; it rejects stale ideologies that confer status upon geographical centres and onto privileged subpopulations while marginalizing others. It is within the realm of art that we can begin to consider the possibility of realizing the ideal polis in a "glocal" way. Art can envisage a polis that may be simultaneously local and global because of the communication that global networks make possible; the polis can extend across the planet. Artists continue to believe and to know that what they do is political. In this way, art continues to be a full participant in realizing social, political, and economic change'.

Concluding this work in June 2022, while there is war in Ukraine, the country having been invaded by Russian military forces, I think the most important document on the Maidan Musem and the Spirit of Maidan is represented by the following lines which were sent to me by Dr IhorPoshyvailo on March 13, 2022. Ihor escaped from Kyiv and found refuge in Lviv. He sent me a video to be presented to a Spanish audience in Murcia. In the video, Ihor is talking clearly about how the war fought in Ukraine is a heritage-cultural war in which the Russian forces want to destroy the cultural past of Ukraine.

Here is the text of the video of Ihor, quoted with his permission.

'The Maidan Museum: Addressing History of the Now. Ladies and Gentlemen, it is my great pleasure to contribute to your remarkable meeting.

Let me start with stressing that it is deeply symbolic to me that great Nelson Mandela ended his earthly life exactly at the time, when Kyiv Euro Maidan Revolution was multiplying its first barricades on the other continent in the heart of Europe. It is as if we took up the symbolic light of Dignity and Rights. Mandela, who is remembered by history as an invincible proponent of freedom and democracy.

According to foreign evaluations of Euromaidan or simply Maidan, a new nation was born in Ukraine, with intrinsic political belief in democracy and liberty.

Maidan has become a project of complete renewal of the state and the system of power, change in world outlook and identity of the nation, and has received a name of the Revolution of Dignity.

Strategically, Ukraine turned its back to its own past, to the Prison of Nations, as USSR used to be called, and turned its face toward the civilized countries by initiating the decolonization process.

The Revolution of Dignity fits in with the world tendency toward so-called velvet, or color revolutions — long-term civil protests demanding democratic reforms and overthrowing of dictatorships yet it is unique in its scale as the biggest pro-European demonstration in the history of the EU. It was the longest mass protest in contemporary history, which lasted ninety-four days non-stop.

The events of the winter 2013 — 2014 in Ukraine demonstrated a social responsibility, a real hunger for civic and community engagement, a burst of cultural activism and deep sacrifice for human democratic values.

In order to commemorate the people killed, the events, and preserve artifacts displaying in different ways the unprecedented movement a number of public initiatives launched a joint project — the Maidan Museum, which has been expanded to the national institution.

A group of cultural activists collected objects and stories from the camp. Many items were taken from the trash and saved from destruction. These preserved evidences will form part of the window into Ukraine and tell more about the protest movement and our cultural identity from prospective of not only historical and dramatic events but bunches of art expressions, creativity, humor and satire as powerful voices and arms of the communities.

Presently the challenge is not only to preserve the collection and make it available for broad public and professionals — for research and reflections, promoting democratic discourse and narratives of freedom. But to turn the Maidan Museum, as an interdisciplinary platform for preserving the memory about the fight for freedom in Ukraine's recent history, into a dialogue and reconciliation institution which will represent multiply points of view and be relevant both in form and content to various audiences and generations.

Strategic assets of the Maidan Museum founded 2016 by the government on the base of the grass-root initiative, are focused on the interests and values of the citizens, since it is all about the memory that museum is trying to preserve, the people who are honored there, thecollections, the ideas that are being generated.

Our institution has three components: a memorial, a museum and an educational center. As of now, Maidan Museum has over four thousand items in its collection including a powerful photo and video archive that constantly grows.

The Museum continues to collect artefacts, documents and oral testimonies. We are open to collaboration with the scholars, students, activists and artists, who are engaged with the concept of a museum as a place for a dialogue, discussions, presentations, commemorative evenings, and screenings.

The Museum's exhibition projects, memorial and educational events and publication are based on the high-quality academic material, the results of research and the best scholarship. Apart from the work of the Registrar and preservation of memorial objects, the Museum staff conducts research of the collections, organizes academic conferences, develops curatorial concepts for expositional and memorial spaces, creates multimedia library, audio and visual archives, carries out field expeditions, collects oral stories, prepares guideline materials, as well as studies different aspects and contexts of the Revolution of Dignity and other revolutions worldwide.

This year we were ready to start construction of the building of the Maidan Museum in the political, cultural and symbolic heart of Ukraine—in it's capital's downtown. But Russian-Ukrainian military conflict expanded by brutal Putin's aggression into a large-scale war in February 24 this year. Now we have not only military, informational and humanitarian frontlines. We have the cultural frontline as Kremlin's missiles, tanks and forbidden by international convention weapons are targeted not only as our land and civil infrastructure, but on our identity, our historical memory, our future as a nation. This is a heritage war. And we have to fight for our past and the future. A few weeks ago, the Maidan Museum addressing history of the now founded the Heritage Emergency

Response Initiative to protect Ukrainian cultural heritage as a part of the world heritage. And we look forward to world support.

In conclusion, let me remind one more symbolic fact. In 1961, Moscow communist leader Khrushchev declared that Russian missiles would destroy Acropolis in Athens if necessary for the achievement of Russian goals. The Greek Prime Minister replied to the Kremlin dictator that Moscow could destroy Acropolis with its weapons, but would never be able to destroy the idea of democracy and persona lfreedom that had been born there. So today, with their courage and determination, with international support, the Ukrainians prove, once again, the truthfulness of this reply.

Glory to Ukraine!

Thank you for your attention and standing with Ukraine!'

Acknowledgements

This academic work has been the result of encounters with exceptional people, without whom there would not have been any research at all. At the beginning of the research, I developed a general idea about the Revolution of Dignity, its real importance, impact, and consequences academic literature and the media, including in particular data on the art produced during the revolution as well as of the conception of the establishment the Ukrainian identity. I therefore embarked on my first visit to Kyiv in 2016 looking for first-hand experiences able to transmit the real meaning of the revolution. The first time I visited the Maidan Square and saw the various pictures commemorating the Heavenly Hundred Heroes was a strong emotional moment. I come from Italy, a European country, and not that distant from Ukraine, but I was faced with the Ukrainian people were really fighting, and being killed for ideals of freedom and dignity, which Europeans often take for granted.

Based on my personal experience I can affirm that during the Cold War the general knowledge in Italy was directed towards the USA, and influenced by USA, while, despite their geographic vicinity, our socio-cultural-political comprehension of the former Warsaw Pact countries and former Soviet Union was very scarce and not stimulated by the education and cultural sectors. NATO was, and still is, a cultural and symbolic system.

Therefore, when the Berlin Wall came down, we only had the vaguest idea of our new neighbours. In Italy we then started to receive the first immigrants from these countries, but our society was impermeable to them, there was no curiosity toward them, we were entrapped in the post Cold War euphoria of the 'winners', and basically there was just glances toward these 'exotic' people and lands. Basically, we were completely ignorant of this part of the world. As a consequence, when in 1992 the Bosnia conflict started at the border of NATO, it was easy for the official western narrative to depict the territory at the East of the NATO border as ghost land, and unfortunately this is still the case, even in high quality journals.

My curiosity, working and academic experiences have brought me to spend years in this 'ghost land', to have contact with people and academics living there, and I can say that a lot of time my 'knowledge' did not overlap with the media images. It was this kind of curiosity who pushed me to visit Kyiv and to look for human experiences, and to record them.

For this reason, I have to thank all the following people, who basically opened my eyes; thanks to all of them, I came away from this experience totally changed.

Therefore, I want to thank the people of the Maidan Museum for their help which has been exceptional. Dr Ihor Poshyvailo (Director Maidan Museum), offered to me the possibility to have an internship at the Museum, which I accepted. Dr Ekateryna Romanova (Head of the Research Department) and Prof. Lesya Onyshko, both of the Maidan Museum, helped me to organize my approach to the topic of the art of Maidan, and the Maidan Museum organized all the meeting and interview with the artists. The people at the 'Information and Exhibition Center of the Maidan Museum' were all helpful and kind, and they did organize an excellent conference for my presentation. I want to thank Victoria Boyko, Nastia Sokyrko, Olga Savenok, Oxana Vara, Olha Salo, Victor Kryvonosov, Yevgenij Safarians, and Yulia Khodorko.

Also, my warm thanks go to the artists who shared their dramatic experiences of the Revolution of Dignity with me, unveiled their creative process; for their human understanding, they represent no less than the soul of my academic research: Oles Kromplias, Tatyana Cheprasova, Taras Kompanichenko, Oleksander Ivanovych Melnyk, Ivan Semesyuk, Sasha Komyakhov, Yuriy Gruzinov, Neda Nedjana, Yulia Ovcharenko, Valery Hladunets, Glib Viches, and Maryna Sochenko.

Dr Alina Ponypaliak took me to a special tour of the National Museum of History of Ukraine (Kyiv) and I am thankful to her for the 'private' lecture she gave me on Ukrainian history which opened my eyes.

Ms Iryna Klishchevskaya, of the Kiev Akademic Theater Koleso, shared with me her experiences of the Revolution of

Dignity and explained to me how some plays talk and presents the Maidan events to the large public.

Ms Dara Sereda, did an outstanding job as the main translator of all my interviews, she accompanied me everywhere, and with me she shared all the strong and painful emotions the informants-interviewees transmitted to us about their experience at the Maidan.

I am grateful to Ms Ksiu Kyrychenko because at the beginning of my research on art and identity in Maidan she mentioned to me the work in progress of the Maidan Museum and put me in contact with the Director of the Maidan Museum.

Dr Chris Farrands read my research, wrote the Foreword, but more importantly, thanks to him and our conversations during my PhD time at Nottingham Trent University (Chris was my supervisor), I started to develop a great interest in Social Anthropology. I have a big intellectual debt toward my friend Chris. Thank you 'Maestro'.

Prof. Gerard Bouchard (Université du Québec, Chicoutimi, Canada) read my work and checked the way I was using his theories, and he gave me his sincere comments on the work I was doing. Thank you.

Dr Frank G. Madsen (Sometime Fellow Commoner, Queens' College, Cambridge, UK) pored over my text and gave me really useful comments. Thank you my friend.

And finally, my friend Prof. Francisco Jarauta (Collège de France, Paris, France) read and provided me with interesting insight of my work. Gracias Paco.

I hope I did not forget to mention anybody, and if I did it, I am really sorry. All the people I met during my experience in Kyiv were kind, helpful, sympathetic and eager to share their experiences with me, thank you to all, I really learnt a lot from all of you.

About the Authors:
Giovanni Ercolani; Chris Farrands

Dr Giovanni Ercolani studied Political Science, Oriental Studies, Art Management and Production, and was awarded a PhD in Social Anthropology with the University of Murcia (Spain) and a PhD in International Relations and Security Studies by the Nottingham Trent University (UK). He is both a Researcher at the 'Society and Culture' Research Group at the University of Murcia (Spain), and a Research Associate at 'LADEC—Laboratoire d'Anthropologie des Enjeux Contemporains' at the Université Lumière Lyon 2 (France), while also an active Thesis Advisor for the 'Peace Operations Training Institute' (USA). Previously, he was lecturer on 'Global Terrorism' and 'Peacekeeping and Conflict Resolution' at the Bilgi University and Yeditepe University in Istanbul (Turkey). Dr Ercolani is member of the Editorial Board of 'The Journal of Security Sciences' (Turkey), and Fellow (elected) of the Royal Anthropological Institute of Great Britain and Ireland (UK); his previous books include the co-edited *Anthropology and Security Studies* (Editum 2013); his papers have been published by, among other outlets, the *Central European Journal of International and Security Studies*; and his multidisciplinary researches focus on the topics of culture, social myths, symbolism, collective imaginaries, identity, and security.

Dr Chris Farrands studied International Relations and Philosophy at the University College of Wales, Aberystwyth and the London School of Economics. He has taught at a number of UK and French Universities and has been a Visiting Professor in universities in Turkey and in Washington DC. He most recently worked as Head of the International Relations team at Nottingham Trent University. Now retired, he continues to publish research and supervise there. He has published widely, including around 100 published articles and papers and eleven edited, single or co-authored books. He is a Fellow of the Royal Society of Arts and of the Royal Anthropological Institute.

Bibliography

Agamben, G. (1998). *Homo Sacer: Sovereign Power and Bare Life.* Standfors, CA: Standford University Press.

Alexander, V. D. (2003). *Sociology of the Arts — Exploring Fine and Popular Forms.* Oxford: Blackwell Publishing.

Alexievich, S. (2017). *Secondhand Time — The Last of the Soviets.* New York: Random House.

Althusser, L. (1988). *Ideologia y aparatos ideologicos de Estado.* Buenas Aires: Ediciones Nueva Vision.

Álvarez Munárriz, Luis (2015). *Categorías Clave de la Antropología.* Sevilla: Signatura Demos.

Anderson. B. (2006). *Imagined Communities: Reflections of the origin and Spread of Nationalism.* London: Verso.

Appadurai, A. (2013). *The Future as Cultural Fact.* London — New York: Verso.

Augé, M. (2009). *Non-Places: An Introduction to Supermodernity.* London: Verso.

Augé, M. (2011). *Straniero di me stesso.* Torino: BollatiBoringhieri.

Augé, M. (2013). *No Fixed Abode –Ethnofictions.* London: Seagull Books.

Bachelard, Gaston (2014). *The Poetics of Space.* Harmondsworth: Penguin.

Balzacq, T. (Ed.) (2011). *Securitization Theory — How Security Problems Emerge and Dissolve.* London and New York: Routledge.

Barthes, R. (2000). *Mythologies.*London: Vintage Books.

Bazzichelli, T. (2006). *Networking. La Rete come arte.* Milano: Costa&Nolan.

Bazzichelli, T. (2013). *Networked Disruption: Rethinking Oppositions in Art, Hacktivism and the Business of Social Networking.* Digital Aesthetics Research Center of the Aarhus University.

Beatty, A. (2019). *Emotional Worlds — Beyond an Anthropology of Emotion.* Cambridge, UK: Cambridge University Press.

Benjamin, W. (1973). *Illuminations.* Bungay, Suffolk: Fontana/Collins.

Berger, J. (2002). *The Shape of a Pocket.* London-Berlin-New York: Bloomsbury.

Berger, John (1972). *Ways of Seeing.* London: Penguin Books.

Berger, P. and Luckmann, T. (1991). *The Social Construction of Reality — A Treatise in the Sociology of Knowledge.* London: Penguin Books.

Bleiker, Roland (ed) (2018). *Visual Global Politics.* London: Routledge.

Bouchard, G. (2017). *Social Myths and Collective Imaginaries*. University of Toronto Press.

Bourdieu, Pierre (1987). *In Other Words*. Stanford, CA: Standford University Press.

Bourdieu, Pierre (2005). *Language&Symbolic Power*. Cambridge: Polity Press.

Burke, Edmund (1998). *A Philosophical Enquiry into the Sublime and the Beautiful; and Other Pre-Revolutionary Writings*. London: Penguin Books.

Buzan, B., Waever, O., de Wilde, J. (1998). *Security: A New Framework for Analysis*. Coulder, CO: Lynne Rienner.

Campbell, J. (1989). *An Open Life: Joseph Campbell in Conversation with Michael Toms*. New York: Harper & Row, Publishers.

Campbell, J. (1991). *The Power of Myth*. New York: Anchor Books.

Canetti, E. (1972). *Massa e Potere*. Milano: Rizzoli.

Cassirer, Ernst (1972). *An Essay on Man*. New Haven and London: Yale University Press.

Crotty, M. (1998). *The foundations of social research: Meaning and perspective in the research process*. Thousand Oaks, CA: Sage.

Dal Lago, A. and Giordano, S. (2006). *Mercanti d'aura – Logiche dell'arte contemporanea*. Bologna: il Mulino.

Durkheim, E. (2001). *The Elementary Forms of Religious Life*. Oxford University Press.

Eco, Umberto (1995). *The Role of the Reader. Explorations in the Semiotics of Texts*. Bloomington: Indiana University Press.

Eco, Umberto (2006). *Lector in Fabula: la cooperazione interpretativa nei testi narrativi*. Milano: Tascabili Bompiani.

Erli, A. and Sommer, R. (eds) (2019). *Narrative in Culture*. Berlin: De Gruyter.

Ercolani, G. (2016). The Anthropological Gaze: Deconstructing the Securitization Process and the Market of Anxiety. In Javier Eloy Martinez Guirao, Baldomero de Maya Sancez, and Anastasia Tellez Infantes (Eds.), *Perspectivas Interdisciplinares en el Estudio de la Culturadìy la Sociedad*. Universidad Miguel Hernandez.

Fagan, Madeleine (2016). *Ethics and Politics after Poststructuralism: Levinas, Derrida and Nancy*. Edinburgh: University of Edinburgh Press.

Farrands, Chris (2000). Language and the possibility of inter-community understanding. *Global Society*, 14, 1: pp. 79-99.

Fierke, K. M. (2007). *Critical Approaches to International Security*. Cambridge: Polity.

Freeland, C. (2001). *But is it Art? – An Introduction to Art Theory*. Oxford University Press.

Fukuyama, F. (2018). *Identity – Contemporary Identity Politics and the Struggle for Recognition*. London: Profile Books.

Galindo Mateo, I., Martin Martinez, J. V. (2007). *Atenea en el Campus – Una aproximacion a las Bellas Artes como disciplina universitaria*. Universidad Politecnica de Valencia.

Galtung, J. (1969). Violence, Peace, and Peace Research. *Journal of Peace Research*, Vol. 6, No. 3, pp. 167-191.

Garcia Canclini, N. (2014). *Art beyond Itself – Anthropology for a Society without a Story Line*. Durham and London: Duke University Press.

Geertz, C. (1973). *The Interpretation of Culture*. New York: Basic Books.

Gombrich, E. H. (1994). *The Story of Art*. London: Phaidon Press Limited.

Hannerz, U. (2010). *Anthropology's World – Life in a Twenty-First –Century Discipline*. London: Pluto Press.

Harris, J. (2008). *Art History – The Key Concepts*. London and New York: Routledge.

Hendry, J. (1999). *An Introduction to Social Anthropology*. London: Palgrave.

Hillman, James (1979). *Il mito dell'analisi*. Milano: Adelphi Edizioni.

Hillman, J. (2019). *Re-visione della psicologia*. Milano: Adelphi Edizioni.

Hryhorczuk, D. (2016). *Myth and Madness*. Maitland, FL: North Loop Books.

Ignatieff, M. (1994). *Blood and Belonging*. London: Vintage.

Jaffe, R. and De Koning, A. (2016). *Introducing Urban Anthropology*. London and New York: Routledge.

Jenkins, R. (2014). *Social Identity*. London and New York: Routledge.

Jociles Rubio, M. I. (1999). Las tecnicas de investigacion en antropologia. Mirada Antropologica y proceso etnografico. *Gazeta de Antropologia*, 15, 1-26.

Kandisky, W. (1977). *Concerning the Spiritual in Art*. New York: Dover Publications, Inc.

Kozak, N. (2017). Art Embedded into Protest: Staging the Ukrainian Maidan. *Art Journal*, 76: 1, 8-27.

Kuhn, Thomas S. (1996). *The Structure of Scientific Revolutions*. Chicago and London: The University of Chicago Press.

Kurkov, A. (2014). *Diari Ucraini*. Rovereto (TN): Keller.

Levi-Strauss, C. (1963). *Structural Anthropology*. Basic Books.

Lisón Tolosana, Carmelo (2012). Rito, funciones y significado. *Música oral del Sur: Música hispana y ritual*, N. 9, pp. 22-28.

Lisón Tolosana, Carmelo (2014). *Antropología – Horizontes Simbólicos.* Valencia: Tirant Humanidades.

Macleod, Alex (2016). La Culture Populaire Visuelle: Un Espace à Explorer Pour Les Études Critiques De Sécurité. *Cultures Et Conflits*, no. 102: 17–32.

Marin, Claire (2017). Penser la souffrance avec Paul Ricouer. *Philosophie*, 132, Janvier 2017, [special edition commemorating Paul Ricoeur], Paris: les editions de minuit, pp. 121-130.

Milhonic, A. (2005). Artivism.At:http://eipcp.net/transversal/1203/milohnic/en/print

Mira, Joan F. (2007). Literatura y antropología. In Carmelo Lisón Tolosana (Ed.), *Introducción a la antropología social y cultural-teoría, método y práctica.* Madrid: Akal.

Moisi, D. (2010). *The Geopolitics of Emotions.* New York: Anchor Books.

Moore, Cerwyn and Farrands, Chris (eds) (2012). *International Relations Theory and Philosophy: Interpretive Dialogues.* London: Routledge, 2nd edition.

Morin, E. (2016). *Sur l'estethique.* Paris: Robert Laffont, Maison des sciences de l'homme.

Moussienko, N. (2016). *Art of Maidan.* Kyiv: Huss.

Mullin, A. (2003). Feminist Art and the Political Imagination. *Hypatia*, Vol. 18, no. 4.

Navarria, D. (2015). *Introduzione all'antropologia simbolica – Eliade, Durand, Ries.* Milano: Vita e pensiero.

Peters, T. (2020). *Sociologia(s) del arte y de las politicas culturales.* Santiago del Chile: metals pesados.

Pinkham, Sophie (2016). *Black Square: Adventures in the Post-Soviet World.* London: William Heinemann.

Plokhy, S. (2012). *The Cossack Myth – History and Nationhood in the Age of Empires.* Cambridge University Press.

Plokhy, S. (2015). *The Gates of Europe – A History of Ukraine.* New York: Basic Books.

Punter, B. (2007). *Metaphor.* London and New York: Routledge.

Rancière, J. (1994). *The Names of History: On the Poetics of Knowledge.* Minneapolis: University of Minnesota Press.

Ranciere, J. (2014). *The Politics of Aestethics – The Distribution of the Sensible.*London: Bloomsbury.

Reid, A. (2015). *Borderland – A Journey Through the History of Ukraine.* London: Weidebfeld & Nicolson.

Ricouer, Paul (1992). *Lecture III, Aux Frontières de la Philosophie, Essais*. Paris: Editions de Seuil.

Ricoeur, Paul (2004). *Memory, History, Forgetting*. Chicago: University of Chicago Press.

Sanmartín Arce, Ricardo (2007). El trabajo de campo. In Carmelo Lisón Tolosana (Ed.), *Introducción a la antropología social y cultural-teoría, método y práctica*. Madrid: Akal.

Sartori, Giovanni (2011). *Logica, metodo e linguaggio nelle scienze sociali*. Bologna: Il Mulino.

Schechner, R. (2003). *Performance Theory*. New York and London: Routledge.

Shubin, Aleksandr (2011). 'The Makhnovist Movement and the national question in the Ukraine 1917-1921', at https://ithanarquista.files. wordpress.com/2017/02/aleksandr-shubin-the-makhnovist-movement.pdf

Stevenson, A. and Waite, M. (Eds.) (2012). *Concise Oxford English Dictionary* (Twelfth Edition). Oxford University Press.

Svasek, M. (2005). The Politics of Chosen Trauma: Expellee Memories, Emotions and Identities. In Kay Milton and Maruska Svasek (Eds.), *Mixed Emotions – Anthropological Studies of Feeling*. Oxford – New York: Berg.

Svasek, M. (2007). *Anthropology, Art and Cultural Production*. London-Ann Arbor, MI: Pluto Press.

Svasek, M. (2008). *Postsocialism – Politics and Emotions in Central and Eastern Europe*. New York – Oxford: Berghahn Books.

Svasek, M. (Ed.). (2012). *Moving Subjects, Moving Objects – Transnationalism, Cultural Production and Emotions*.New York – Oxford: Berghahn Books.

Tejeda Martin, I. (2006). *El montaje expositivo como traduccion – fidelidades, traiciones y hallazgos en el arte contemporaneo desde los anos 70*. Madrid: Trama editorial.

Torbakov, I. (2018). *After Empire: Nationalist Imagination and Symbolic Politics in Russia and Eurasia in the Twentieth and Twenty-First Century*. Stuttgart: ibidem-Verlag.

Volkan, V. (1999). *Bloodlines: From Ethic Pride to Ethnic Terrorism*. Boulder, CO: Westview.

Volkan, V. (2004). *Blind Trust – Large Groups and Their Leaders in Times of Crisis and Terror*. Charlottesville, Virginia: Pitchstone Publishing.

Volkan, V. (2006). *Killing in the Name of Identity – A Study of Bloody Conflicts*. Charlottesville, Virginia: Pitchstone Publishing.

Wilson, B. (2020). *Metropolis — A History of the City, Humankind's Greatest Invention*. London: Vintage.

Womack, M. (2005). *Symbols and Meaning — A Concise Introduction*. Oxford: Altamira Press.

Webpages: Novinkiblog (2016). 'History of the Now — a museum for Maidan. An Interview with Ihor Poshyvailo'. at: https://novin kiblog.wordpress.com/2016/02/14/history-of-the-now-a-museum-for-maidan-an-interview-with-ihor-poshyvailo/

Index